ONLY CHILD

EDITED BY

Deborah Siegel and Daphne Uviller

HARMONY BOOKS • NEW YORK

ONLY CHILD

WRITERS ON THE
SINGULAR JOYS
AND SOLITARY SORROWS OF
GROWING UP SOLO

Published in the United States by Harmony Books, an imprint of the
Crown Publishing Group, a division of Random House, Inc., New York.
www.crownpublishing.com

Harmony Books is a registered trademark and the Harmony Books colophon
is a trademark of Random House, Inc.

Library of Congress Cataloging-in-Publication Data
Only child : writers on the singular joys and solitary sorrows of
growing up solo / edited by Deborah Siegel and Daphne Uviller.—1st ed.
1. Only child. I. Siegel, Deborah. II. Uviller, Daphne.
HQ777.3.P37 2006
306.874—dc22   2005037757

ISBN-13: 978-0-307-23806-1
ISBN-10: 0-307-23806-7

Printed in the United States of America

Design by Chris Welch

10   9   8   7   6   5   4   3   2   1

First Edition

To Renée and Allen Siegel, and Rena and Richard Uviller,
our gratitude.

Contents

ONLY CHILD

INTRODUCTION

Party of One

WHAT'S IT *LIKE* being an only child? We, the sibling-free, have been asked this question throughout our lives. It started during childhood, as playmates wailed over decapitated Barbies whose heads had been repurposed as emergency replacement parts for their brothers' Transformers sets. It continued in adolescence, when friends shared a litany of complaints against trespassing, teasing, diary-reading brothers and sisters. As adults, we're grilled by our peers, many of whom are marrying later and anxiously contemplating a single go at reproduction. Do *we* think they should have a second? Did *we* turn out lonely, spoiled, socially inept, or otherwise freakish? If they can't have a second, do *we* think they should head for a test tube or adopt a companion for Junior?

A couple of years ago, two only children were taking up space at a café, making one coffee stretch out over an afternoon, pondering such questions. We had stumbled into a debate about the pros and cons of being an "only," a status Daphne realized she loved when she thought about it at all. The center of attention, the recipient of all things monetary, and the sole occupant of her bedroom—a veritable real-estate triumph when you're raised in New York City—Daphne recalled actual nightmares about her mother announcing she was pregnant.

Deborah, on the other hand, had a more conflicted relationship with her only-child status. She often felt *too* much the center of attention, envied the automatic playmates enjoyed by her best friend, the youngest of six, and felt apprehensive about preferring to hang with the grown-ups. She dreamed about the day her parents would return from one of her mother's fertility surgeries with the announcement that Mommy was pregnant with number two.

As we compared notes on being the main axis around which our parents revolved, we began to realize that being an only child had—dare we say it?—existential implications. Do onlies have special insight about what it means to fly solo? What it means to be the sole repository of your family's gene pool? Isn't the only child simply the most exaggerated version of all of us, navigating life alone?

And then there were the less existential (but equally gripping) questions. Are onlies spoiled? Lonely? Is there a difference between those of us whose parents chose to have only one child and those whose parents tried desperately for a repeat performance but couldn't achieve it? Are we more poised because we were raised among grown-ups, or are we insufferable, pompous know-it-alls who think the sun rises and sets on us? Do we make unreasonable demands on our romantic partners, expecting them to give us the attention our parents gave us growing up? Do we know how to love more than one child if we ourselves have a litter? Who will be there to help us care for our aging parents when the tides turn?

It's not just navel-gazing that drives our interest in the subject, we swear. Our numbers are ever increasing. There are an estimated 15 million only children in the United States alone, and the number of single-child families is on the rise. Over the past twenty years, the percentage of women nationwide who have one child has more than doubled, from 10 percent to more than 23 percent. Single-child families are the fastest-growing families in this country and in most industrialized western European countries as well. Historically, during tough economic times, we see an increase in only-borns, and that is exactly what seems to be happening today. In other words, when the market goes down, the number of spaces available at your local preschool goes up.

Only childhood in the United States at the dawn of the new millennium raises a number of culturally specific questions. Among the environmentally conscious, many question whether global overcrowding creates a moral imperative to create more onlies here at home. And while Americans continue to express outrage over China's forced one-child policy, increasingly we seem voluntarily to be abiding by that policy ourselves, in part because American women are marrying later and later. As deferred childbearing becomes increasingly common, are stereotypes about having a single child beginning to emerge? With dual-income parents now the norm, do latchkey or nanny-raised only children feel a particular isolation? When two onlies marry in this era of inadequate health care, whose aged parents are taken in first?

Okay, but what's it *like?*

You could read the myriad books out there about how to avoid raising a spoiled only brat. Or you could study the lives of numerous celebrity onlies, dead and alive, real and fictional, from Sinatra to Superman, from beautiful Natalie Portman to biblical Noah. Did the Man of Steel have trouble sharing? Did the builder of the ark board all those animals because he was lonely as an only? But wait—are they really the right onlies to look to for insights? We think not.

This book lets onlies who are masters and mistresses of the written word answer the question, in distinctive voices, and with unwavering candor. Who better than writers to tell tales of onliness from the perspective we all seek—*the inside?* Who better to contemplate the continuum of solitude on the page?

As we sought out scribes, we found that identifying sibling-free writers was an indirect, often clumsy, and frequently absurd undertaking. We would *hear* that a particular writer was an only, and we'd shoot him or her an e-mail. Because of their polite responses, we now know that Jonathan Ames, Jhumpa Lahiri, and Ha Jin are definitely not onlies. And Michael Chabon, in case you were curious, is one of six.

Other writers confirmed that they were onlies, but just couldn't risk alienating the only two people they called family. One told us she'd have to wait until both her parents were six feet under before she could write anything at all about her life. Others, like John Updike, felt they had already addressed the topic repeatedly in their fiction, by making their protagonists sibling-free. Others waffled, because the task was difficult: "Hard to separate the only from the childhood," said one. Many pointed out the irony of this entire book: It's an impossible task to know if you are the way you are because you are without siblings. Or, as one contributor put it, "It's a little bit like a trout saying, 'Water: works for me.'"

No matter. We got our group. So *is* there anything that each and every one of the onlies whose stories are recorded here has in common? They are all extraordinary writers. Is there anything that each and every one of them has in common because they are only children?

We've asked these essayists to reflect on transformative episodes that defined them as only children. For some, their epiphanies came early, during childhoods populated with hovering parents and fleets of imaginary friends. For others, crystallizing moments occurred later, in sterile hospital halls while caring for a parent with cancer. For still others, those moments came sometime in between, taking shape around experiences of dating, mating, or becoming a parent themselves. For many, awareness of their only-child status is constant. As kids, they rarely rebelled, and as adults, they continue to talk to their parents every day, their desire and obligation to do so melding into a single, blurred compulsion. That sense of obligation sometimes reaches unusual heights; as one writer puts it, "I knew I couldn't die." Their insights are grouped into four life stages: childhood, finding love and friendship, becoming parents, and becoming orphaned, alone.

In Part I, "Singular Sensations," some writers describe what it's like to grow up doubly alone, the solo child of divorce or of a young single mother or of a single father dying of AIDS. Others describe growing up only in the city, where only children are common, others in the burbs, where single-child families are less the norm. Some writers recall being unnaturally entwined with their parents, while others tell tales of near neglect. While some cherished their time home alone, others were painfully lonely and ashamed of their families' tiny size. Feeling like misfits, they lurked hungrily around the chaos of big clans, imagining themselves as orphans on the sidelines, searching for clues on kidspeak. Some longed for a sibling—one was so desperate, she launched a campaign to adopt a chimp—and when none was forthcoming, they found ersatz siblings: Santa Claus, Peter and Jane (British cousins of Dick and Jane), neighbors, even a postcard collection. Others knew they had a great racket going, prizing their peaceful solitude and their parents' attention above all else. Two writers go so far as to compare single-child families to the height of civilization.

In Part II, "We Are . . . Family," two writers discovered the hard way that water is indeed thinner than blood; their attempts to turn their friends into family left them hurt, disappointed, and bereft. Others describe what it's like to crave solitude like a drug and to find friendships all the more gratifying for being able to leave them at the end of a rendezvous. Some explore the ways that finding love challenged the equilibrium of their original trio. They struggle under the weight of being all that their parents have, even as they grow up and away. They tell tales of reluctant separations, overly vigilant parents, and the sticky logistics of switching your "emergency contact" when you marry. Some found themselves dating by committee, no tryst complete until rehashed with Mom and Dad.

In Part III, "A Sib for Junior?" when it comes to parenting and deciding how many children to have, a couple of writers who loved growing up solo have decided to deprive their own children of the experience for insurance purposes; a triangular family cannot afford to lose one of its legs. They turn the tables on the stereotype, framing "deprivation" as an absence of onliness rather than an absence of sibs. But they also worry how they will learn to spread love among multiples.

Finally, in Part IV, "Still Only After All These Years," writers who have lost a parent grapple with the terrifying liberty of having no fellow historians; what is your past, subjected to the fickleness of memory, with no sibling to hold you in check? They urge fellow onlies to "get it down on paper," to record their family life before it is too late—which is exactly what they do here.

These essays proffer fresh language and a new vocabulary with which to make sense of some of our mutual experiences as only children: "only adulthood," "habitual enmeshment," "a longing for neglect." They do the near impossible, imagining what life might have been like had things been otherwise. Writes Elizabeth DeVita-Raeburn, who lost a brother and became an only child, "How can you gauge the depth with which the people we love and live with leave their traces in you—after the fact, or hypothetically? That's what we're all searching for, those of us wistful onlies, in these essays, in one way or another."

Whether you're an only out to discover how your experience compares to others, a parent or spouse of an only, a parent pondering whether to stop at one, or someone with siblings who's always wondered how the other half lives, these writers will answer all the questions you never even thought to ask. They air dirty laundry, reveal singular joys, and get to the root of the mystique. More than mere stories of birth order and head counts, these essays grapple with questions about love, loss, solitude, and the longing for human connection. In the pages ahead, these twenty-one sage scribes sans sibs will make you laugh, cry, and sigh with relief—and maybe even make you feel fleeting pangs of envy.

We hope you enjoy the party.

I

SINGULAR
SENSATIONS

Childhood

Postcards to Myself

Peter Terzian

WHEN I WAS in second grade, I brought home books from my elementary-school library with titles like *Fair Is Our Land* and *Beyond New England Thresholds*. These books had glossy pictures of colonial towns with sheep grazing in the commons and forts where cannons were fired on the hour. I pleaded to be taken to these places, to monuments, writers' homes, battlefields, and living-history museums. I planned prospective itineraries on road maps and selected appropriately priced motels from our *AAA Guide*. I had no brothers and sisters whose wishes needed to be taken into account. How could my parents refuse?

We were a family of four: my mother, my father, me, and my mother's mother, who moved in with us not long after I was born. I grew up thinking of my grandmother as a sort of surrogate sibling. I was her only grandson, and she doted on me, pouring my cereal each morning and picking up my toys every evening. When I came home from school, we would sit together on the lumpy couch in the den and watch children's public television shows. But my mother and father didn't invite my grandmother to join us on our vacations, and she didn't ask to come along. Perhaps there was a silent understanding that travel allowed my parents and me to revert temporarily to our original, two-generational state. We became a family of three.

On the road, I would sit alone in the back of the car, surrounded by pillows and books and stuffed animals. There was no one to fight with, no one to draw an invisible do-not-cross line down the middle of the seat with, no one to play billboard lotto with. Still, I didn't miss having a sibling. My parents were up front, taking turns behind the wheel and reading the newspaper. We all looked out the windows at the passing landscape. I read out loud descriptions of the attractions we'd soon be seeing, from brochures that I had written away for months in advance. I rode in a bubble of contentment, happy to be away from my school and our street and our small domestic worries. Still, I counted the hours until our arrival— how long it would take to check in to our hotel, how long before we came across a souvenir stand, how long before I spotted a rack of postcards.

I BOUGHT MY first postcards on our first family vacation, a long weekend in Washington, D.C. It was 1975, and I was feverish with the American Bicentennial. Every morning, I stood at the livingroom window and recited the Pledge of Allegiance to the flag in our next-door neighbor's yard. I sang patriotic songs around the house and wore a plastic tricornered hat at the dinner table. I helped my parents pick out wallpaper for my bedroom—a pattern of colonial cartography. It was my greatest wish to visit the District of Columbia. I wanted to see the marble of the Capitol building shining like polished teeth. I wanted to walk the Mall.

My parents were only too happy to grant this wish. My mother was a childhood bookworm. My father was a second-generation Armenian-American who grew up with other children of immigrants. English-language books were scarce in his early life, and his parents placed little value on education. His father told him that he should take up a trade. But the GI Bill allowed my father to go to college, and he became a high-school math teacher. His great hope was that his son would be a scholar. And now, here I was, begging for a trip that most kids my age would have thought perilously close to schoolwork.

We drove to Washington, a seven-hour trip from our home in upstate New York. At the Jefferson Memorial, we admired the statue of the president. I read aloud the inscriptions on the walls, excerpts of his letters and writings; some of these passages I already knew by heart. My father's face showed boundless pride as I precociously sounded out the long words: tyranny . . . inalienable . . . providence . . .

I was to be rewarded. Taking me by the hand, my father led me down a staircase to a souvenir shop in the basement. There he brought me to a white pegboard display, with rows of little wire racks that held thick stacks of small, brilliantly colored pictures. These were postcards, my father explained. Did I want any, to keep as mementos?

I wanted many, and I wanted them badly. Together we picked out about a dozen: the district's rotundas and pillared porticoes; the Washington Monument, that alien-looking obelisk; cherry blossoms surrounding the Tidal Basin; aerial views of the green-and-white city. One card was a grid of about twenty miniature scenes, a post-card like a quilt of smaller postcards. (This was soon to become my most cherished specimen.) My father handed a dollar—all this for a single dollar!—to the kindly white-haired woman behind the counter. I clasped the bag of postcards for the rest of the day until it was wrinkled and fuzzy with the sweat from my hands.

Back at the hotel, I fingered the scalloped edges of these cards; they were shaped like rectangular pieces of lace. Each had a white bar across the bottom that identified in elegant script the subject of the picture. The skies were deep blue, bluer than any real sky, with cottony clouds. The buildings and monuments sparkled. The places in these photographs were like none I had ever seen. I wanted to enter these pictures, where everything was perfect. I imagined living inside a postcard.

When we returned home a few days later, I showed the post-cards to my grandmother. She gave me a clear plastic shoe box, embossed with a pattern of daisies and topped with a butter-yellow lid, to store them in. I placed the box on a shelf above my desk and admired the cards through the transparent flowers. There were too few postcards for such a long box; they fell over any time I moved it. It was clear to me that I needed to fill the box.

OVER TIME MY collection grew steadily. One spring, we took a trip to Florida, to Walt Disney World and south to Miami, with stops at roadside attractions in between. In gift shops, I skipped over postcards of bikinied women on generic-looking beaches and found parrots and pyramids of rapturous water-skiers. We spent a long weekend in Boston, following the Freedom Trail in a pelting rainstorm that inverted our umbrellas, my accumulating packets of postcards sheltered deep under my layers of coat and sweater. We trekked across the state to Niagara Falls, the banks thick with honky-tonk shops and wax museums that I found wildly alluring.

My parents were supportive of my new habit. Postcard hoarding was inexpensive and educational; what was there to object to? My collecting impulse was abetted by my grandmother, who belonged to a local senior-citizens group. The seniors went on "mystery trips" every few months. I was fascinated by the idea of older people boarding a bus for a day's excursion, not knowing where they were going until they were on the highway, when the group organizer would announce their destination. These places never sounded very exciting—a large shopping mall on the outskirts of a run-down city, an old-fashioned general store that sold jam and wicker items. But when my grandmother returned in the evening, she always had two or three additions for my postcard box.

I fiddled with my cards obsessively. I would bring the box out to the front porch and sit on a folding lawn chair, flipping through them. I would count them, then count them again. My father gave me a set of index-card dividers, which I used to separate them into geographic categories. I was a child; naturally, I wanted to *play* with my postcards. But I knew that the neighborhood kids my age didn't play like this. No one else had this sort of toy.

I decided to write on one. The blank spaces on the backs beckoned. I turned over the best one, the multipictured card from Washington. Who could I write to? I couldn't think of anyone; I would write to myself. "Dear Peter," I began. Then I paused—I had nothing to say. I put the card back, ashamed. I had marred my prized possession. Later, I would wince whenever I came across the childish scrawl.

Sometimes I glimpsed the difference between my world—my solitude, my unique live-in grandparent, my idiosyncratic obsessions—and the other world, the world of nuclear families, of brothers and sisters. Next door to us lived Josh and Jenny, twins two years older than me, who lived in a house of shared toys and board games. I wondered, Did the whole family play these games together after dinner, like they did on Saturday morning television commercials? I tried to cajole my family into sitting down to Monopoly or Clue. But my grandmother couldn't understand the rules, or my father would grow restless. "I don't like board games," he would say with a grin, relishing the coming pun. "They *bore* me."

One day I heard the twins talking about how they were going to make paper masks that evening with their parents in preparation for a church youth-group event. I thought longingly about the mask-making all afternoon. When it grew dark I pulled a book of craft projects from my bookcase and crossed the lawn between the two houses. Jenny answered the bell. "I have this book, it might have instructions for how to make masks," I explained. "We don't need it," she said. I put one foot up on the doorjamb, as if to inch my way into the house. "What are you *doing?*" she asked icily. She closed the door in my face, pushing me back onto the porch.

I came to realize there were things I could do outside the house and things I could only do inside. Outside, I tried to join other kids in made-up games of War and Spaceship, making machine-gun and siren sounds. Inside, I quietly tended my postcards like a garden.

This division, unfortunately, wasn't always so neat. I knew, for example, that I couldn't bring my postcard box to school. But for a while, I would stash a few cards into a large blue zippered pencil case. I didn't dare take them out; rather, when I was in need of comfort in the middle of class, I would pretend that I needed a new or different pencil, and peek in the bag at the hidden image.

WHEN I TURNED ten, my parents and I took a monthlong trip to California. My collection nearly doubled. So many new attractions: giant trees! Cable cars! My father's second cousin, a pistachio farmer outside of Fresno, invited us to stay at his ranch for a month; he and his wife and their two daughters, who were a few years my senior, traveled with us up and down the state. Kristi and Katrina were at first curious about my interest. They even began picking out cards here and there for themselves. But as the weeks went by and the long hours in the family's VW van wore everyone down, my obsession became an annoyance. I would spot a display of postcards on the sidewalk outside a cheap souvenir store and bring the clan to a halt while I squeaked the revolving rack around, hunting for fresh Kodachrome. My cousins blew at their bangs and tapped the toes of their clogs to dramatize their impatience.

LATER THAT YEAR, when we moved to a new neighborhood, I refused to pack my postcards with my toys and books. Instead, I sat in the cab of the moving truck on the way to the new house with my shoe box in my lap. I had a new favorite card that I proudly displayed through the transparent front of the box. The words "Greetings from the Golden State" were emblazoned over a triptych of the Sacramento Statehouse, the Golden Gate Bridge, and Half Dome.

That fall, as I entered junior high school, I grieved over our

California trip. I tried desperately to recapture it. In English class, I wrote a poem about horseback riding in Yosemite. ("The horse / clopped / on the beaten path / far behind / the tour group.") At home, I decided to compose my life's story. The first chapter was a day-by-day recounting of our month in California. ("We drove along the Pismo state beach for about twenty minutes. We had dinner at McDonald's. I had a banana shake. The next day we checked out of our motel.") I started a second chapter that began with my birth and proceeded chronologically from there, but I quickly lost interest. The non-California periods of my life didn't seem so exciting anymore.

My parents bought a small business that took up much of their time. We didn't go on many vacations anymore. I was growing older and fitting into my new body awkwardly. My feet hurt, my posture was bad, my rear end stuck out. I didn't know what clothes to wear. My glasses, Coke-bottle lenses in aviator frames, were usually covered in dust and dandruff. I was confused about music. The junior-high-school walls were tattooed in blue pen with strange logos—ZoSo, AC/DC. I only knew that these had something to do with devilish bands led by hairy men.

I became a walking target for jocks and burnouts. I was afraid to use the boys' room. I wished I had an older sibling, a sister with long straight hair, who would tell me what clothes to buy and what music to listen to. She would miraculously swoop in to fend off any would-be tormentors.

But what if I had a sister who became a jock or a burnout herself? What if she joined the ranks of my tormentors? I imagined an additional presence in our small suburban home, another person's voice and smells; long hair in the sink. She would be all-seeing, all-knowing. And I would be self-conscious about playing with postcards in front of her. She might make fun of them. Worse, she might tell my classmates about them.

I entertained a more horrific thought: She might actually *like* my postcards and want to play with them herself. What if she mishandled them? Or left them out in the backyard? Or got peanut butter on them?

I grew increasingly nostalgic for past trips. I longed to be elsewhere, far from home and school, secure with my parents, seeing new sights, breathing different air. We weren't traveling, but I searched for more postcards. At the stationery store in the mall, I'd buy cards of our city and the minor points of interest nearby: a bridge just outside of town, named after a Polish Revolutionary War general, on the highway to the Canadian border; bicyclists in a dull-looking park by the river; the large plaster dog, a local landmark, on the roof of an old hi-fi factory.

I stayed home from school more and more, coaxing myself into sore throats and "stomach problems." I would lie on the couch like an invalid, and my grandmother would set up a TV tray beside me on which I perched my postcard box. I studied each card over and over again. I would assemble a group into a sequence and relive an itinerary: We crossed into Canada on *this* bridge; we first saw the falls from *here;* we stayed at a hotel on *this* hill; we boarded the little boat *there.*

My parents sensed my restlessness. We tried a few more car trips, but something wasn't the same. We drove along the New England coast, but we fought over where to stay, what to eat, and I sat in the backseat crying in frustration. We drove to Hershey Park, but my parents couldn't go on the rides—my mother's bad back, my father's high blood pressure. So I went on the flumes and roller coasters by myself, the single passenger paired with the unhappy fifth wheel of another group.

At home, there was no one to play with. I had some friends at school who also fell between social sets, who were timid or unathletic and tried not to stand out. Every Sunday at church school, I saw the Armenian-American friends—children of my father's childhood friends—whom I had known all my life. But I couldn't figure out how to convert these acquaintances into after-school visits or bike rides. I knew no one in our new neighborhood. One street over, there were some older boys, but they had welcomed me with a pelting of snowballs at the school-bus stop.

Time hung heavy on my hands. Always, I returned to my postcards. I needed to *do* something with them, to busy myself with them. I picked out some of my favorites—the House of the Seven Gables, a mall in Fresno, the dolphin show at a nearby amusement park—and taped them into a scrapbook. I wasn't happy with the result. I tried to take them out again, but when I peeled the tape off the back it left fuzzy tear marks. I kept running my fingers over the shredded paper, as if I could heal the postcards by touch.

One night I brought the box of cards into the empty living room. I took them out, one by one, placing them side by side on the carpet, like a mosaic. I liked the effect. Pictures everywhere. A sea of houses, mountains, monuments. Soon I ran out of space. There was nowhere to step. I stopped and looked out the picture window at the darkening street, but all I could see was my own reflection. I was standing awkwardly in the middle of an illuminated room, balanced on tiptoe over a floor covered with postcards.

I imagined other twelve-year-olds in other houses, on streets beyond mine, doing normal things. All across town, my classmates were having long telephone conversations with one another. Boys my age were biking home to schoolwork and siblings and games.

I flushed with shame. Anyone walking by could look in the window and see me. What if someone from school saw me? What if one of the boys on the next block passed by?

I went into the kitchen, where my parents were sitting at the table, sharing their evening ritual of newspapers and sugar-free ice cream. I pulled a black trash bag out from under the sink. I walked back into the living room and started to tear my postcards in half, first singly, then in twos and threes, then fistfuls. Within ten minutes, I had torn up each one. The bag was full. I went through the kitchen and out to the garage. I put the bag full of postcard pieces into one of the bins.

I returned to the kitchen and sat down with my parents.

"I tore up my postcards," I said.

My mother's mouth fell open. *"What?"* She put down her newspaper.

My father made a face that was part confusion, part disgust. "You did *what?*"

"I tore up my postcards. I was sick of them, so I tore them up."

"Aw, Jesus." He put down his spoon. "Why would you do a thing like that?"

"I don't know," I said. "I just felt like it."

"All of those lovely postcards," my mother said.

I sat there smiling stupidly.

For days afterward, they seemed wary, as if they weren't sure what I would do next.

I RATTLED AROUND the house like a loose marble for the next few years, picking up new interests—jigsaw puzzles, trivia books— and then dropping them. In the evenings, I sat at the foot of my grandmother's bed and we watched her small television. We liked comedies about nuns. Our favorite was a made-for-TV movie, a caper in which a nun had to jump from a tall ledge into a fireman's rescue net.

I had a hard time paying attention in the classroom. I got B minuses. Outside of the classroom, I struggled to fit in. I saw other boys wearing rugby shirts, so I wore those, too. If there was a situation where I might say something funny, I tried to quote some TV show I had seen. But my timing was all wrong. I mumbled, and no one understood a word I said.

ONE DAY, MIDWAY through my junior year of high school, I was sitting at a table in the school library. Some seniors whom I didn't know asked to share the table. One of them, a boy named Mike, started joking around with me. He asked me what music I liked. I named some bands I had seen on MTV that seemed all right. He said they sucked. But he said this in such a friendly way that I wasn't hurt.

I sat with Mike and his friends again a few days later. When I saw him in the hallways between classes, I'd stop to talk. One evening, the phone rang. It was Mike. He was depressed. A girl he liked didn't like him back. I took this very seriously, offered consolation and advice. I tried to act as though I had conversations like this all the time. But I was secretly thrilled.

My transformation must have been gradual, a relentless mental notation of social habits and mannerisms that took me years to put into effect. Still, from then on I pinpointed a date—the day when Mike sat at my library table—as when I truly entered the world. I compensated for a long period of loneliness, throwing myself into my new social life at hurricane force.

By senior year, my calendar was perpetually booked. After school: have an early dinner with Doug at the Ponderosa Steakhouse, visit Kathy at the dried-fruit-and-nut stand at the mall, shop for clothes with Bob and Bruce at the army-navy store. At night: rush through homework, work my way down my list of phone numbers, write letters to older friends who had left for college. Weekends: borrow Rickie Lee Jones records from Tristi, go to a Merchant Ivory film with Tina and Carolyn, drive around with Nick until midnight. In the summer, I threw cookouts for my friends in my backyard. I heard that some girls liked me. I went on a date with one, to see a Goldie Hawn movie. A girl from my English class named Theresa told me that I was her second choice for a prom date—her first choice had accepted, but still I was happy.

I found a job scooping ice cream at the local Friendly's and became close to a red-headed coworker named John, a music student at a local college. I realized that there was a unique quality, something heightened, about my feelings for him. One day we made plans to go to the local army-navy store. I drove to his house to pick him up. He had to change his clothes, he said, and went into his bedroom. When he came out a minute later, he was putting on a new shirt. His fingers were halfway through fastening the buttons, and I could see the pink skin of his upper chest. *Don't look,* I told myself. *Go ahead, look,* another voice said. *Look while you've got the chance.*

I often wondered which of these friends was my *best friend,* an appellation that changed frequently. After a particularly good phone conversation, I would decide that Nick was really my best friend. A few weeks later, I'd spend an afternoon listening to tapes in Dave's room: No, it was actually Dave who was my best friend. I was searching for some mysterious, lasting attachment—a substitute for the sibling bond I never had and the romantic relationship I had yet to have.

The spring before my graduation, my father and I traveled to Germany, to visit the family of one of his childhood friends. I had never been abroad, and I was excited. Also anxious: I worried about everything changing back home, my social world evaporating in the ten days that I would be gone.

Germany was disappointing. My father's friend lived in a small hilly town famous for a Baroque château and a porcelain factory. Our travels outside the town were limited—we couldn't speak German and found it difficult to master the train system. I was grumpy with my father. Still, I took the journey as an opportunity to shower my friends back home with gifts. On the town's main shopping street, I bought them Swiss Army knives and new-wave records you couldn't find at our local mall.

At a stationery store I collected a stack of postcards. Back in my small room at the family's home, I wrote messages on each one, to John and Tristi and Tina and Dave. I used all the phrases that I knew people used on postcards—"Wish you were here" and "See you next week." And on a walk later that afternoon I dropped them into a mailbox.

I'm My Own Grandpa

Molly Jong-Fast

I HAVE ALWAYS been thrilled about my lack of a sibling for two reasons. One, my parents are horrible parents (nice people, snappy dressers, talented writers, funny jokesters, attractive dancers, but horrible parents). Actually, that's not really true; my parents aren't horrible parents, but the truth is much less verbally attractive than that: My parents are complicated people, my mother weirdly hot and cold from a lifetime with my psychotic grandma, and my father complicated in his own way from a lifetime with his psychotic father, Communist hero Howard Fast. The second reason I have always been thrilled about my lack of a sibling? Inheritance, inheritance, and inheritance.

Sadly, my joy seems completely lost on my mother, who is always apologizing for my state of siblinglessness.

"We were always going to have more children," my mother confided in me one snowy morning in Weston, Connecticut. We were sitting at the window in the kitchen in our pajamas.

I smiled into my coffee. I had explained countless times that I was happy as an only, but since she seemed never to hear that, I played along. "Sure, why not?"

Mom was in confessional mode, and nothing, not even a cadre of Symbionese Liberation Army guerrillas, could stop her. "No, really, I always wanted more children."

Mom's current groundskeeper was out in the woods practicing Wicca with her lesbian lover. Alger Hiss (as I will call the caretaker for the rest of this essay) had been causing me a bit of worry for the last few months. I had recently found a huge outdoor kiln that was filled with the carcasses of rather unlucky squirrels (I say "rather" not as a pretentious mannerism but merely as a counterbalance; after all, who am I to say that this life is preferable to the squirrel afterlife?).

But what did this have to do with having more children? Was it the lesbian Wicca-practicing Alger Hiss who had caused Mummy to lose interest in procreating, or was it something more?

True, Mom was no stranger to lesbians, snow, or Wicca. I still believed as a family we could probably do better with a more conventional groundskeeper, or just one who could shop for groceries instead of murdering squirrels. This is not to say that I like squirrels. Rats with tails are one of the few things I truly loathe, along with the poetry of Jewel and the predictions of one Jackie Stallone, psychic to the stars (and Nancy Reagan). But where was I?

"I guess you could say it was our divorce that screwed us in the procreating department. If you will excuse the double entendre."

How could I not excuse the double entendre? I was the daughter of the queen of erotica; I understood what it meant to be screwed by screwing (as my mother's first novel had cast a huge penislike shadow over all of us). "I could see how that might cause problems," I said.

"But I always thought being an only child ruined you."

"Thanks, Mom."

"No, really. I think it made you hopelessly spoiled."

"Thanks, Mom, for all the support."

"No, it's true. Siblings would have taught you how to share."

"But I kind of have siblings. I have my two half brothers and my one stepsister, and let's not forget my three teenage uncles."

Mom said nothing; she just looked out the window in horror. Running across the snow-covered lawn was a huge naked lesbian, her enormous breasts bouncing—*boom, boom, boom.*

She was, of course, not our lesbian groundskeeper, nor was she my lesbian aunt, nor was she my lesbian best friend. She was just yet another friend of Alger Hiss.

I looked at Mom. "I don't understand why anyone would get implants."

Mom's horror was quickly replaced by a need to proselytize her feminist values. To Mom (as with many baby-boomer women) everything was an opportunity to brainwash me with her self-love and her "I'm okay, you're okay" shtick. "You know what upsets me the most about you and your generation?"

"What?"

"The self-loathing."

"Oy vey."

"We burned our bras so that you could respect your womanhood and understand that the female body is beautiful."

"So beautiful, yes. Tell me the ménage à trois story again?"

Mom smiled, slightly embarrassed. "It was the seventies then."

"Yes, but that hardly makes it okay that you and a certain man whom I call Dad had a sexual encounter with a certain lesbian author who now has a haircut that looks a lot like the flattop MC Hammer sported in the eighties."

"That's not even true," Mom said.

"Do-do-do-do hammer time do-do-do! Hammer time! Hammer, don't hurt 'em."

"I never."

"Do-do-do-do."

But I am getting distracted by my own obsession with lesbians with enormous breasts. Okay, that's a little worrying. Where was I? Yes, I am an only child. And as an only child I am writing an essay for a book filled with essays about how special and different we only children are. And while most of the contributors to this book are special, different, and immensely talented, I am none of these things, unless you consider me special in a kind of Special Olympics kind of way—which, by the way, isn't funny at all (and I apologize from the bottom of my heart to all of my readers who are special in that way).

Anyway, when I was a little girl I loved *The Muppet Show*. It was my favorite show. There was one song that I particularly loved. It was called "I'm My Own Grandpa," and it was about a miner who had married his cousin and the cousin had married his aunt or something and somehow he had ended up as his own grandpa. Now I know this is supposed to be an essay about the general plight of the only child. And yes, I am an only child, but I am one freaky only child. Not quite my own grandpa, but damn close.

It all started with a guy named Moses and some people called the Jews. These people walked through the Red Sea with unleavened bread on their backs because they didn't have time for the bread to rise. This bread became Eli Zabar's flat bread and it was sold in all the Vinegar Factories and all the other E.A.T. stores throughout New York City and the Hamptons.

Okay, I guess I'll speed it up a bit. My parents married and divorced soon after. This is where the fun part starts. Dad married Barbara. Barbara was a DA. But, sadly, she didn't get to carry a gun. Though she did once put me in jail, for fun, as a joke, a cute joke. I started crying. Luckily, in twenty-three short years of therapy I can almost talk about the incident without wetting myself and curling into a ball.

Mom hated Barbara because Dad had married her. Dad hated Mom because Mom had married him. Mom hated Dad because he had married her. And then Mom got with Dart. Then the police got to Dart and then soon after Jesus got to Dart and Dart started selling meat from a truck, then Mom married Ken. So where do the siblings come in, you, ask? After all, isn't this an essay about being an only child?

Yes, the siblings! My stepmother produced two adorable heirs to the Howard Fast legacy of irritable bowel syndrome and pathological lying. Yes, I have two little half brothers—Ben and Dan, both lovely and adorable, neither with irritable bowel syndrome or a penchant for the whole not-truth. These two boys are so perfect (tall, good looking, non-neurotic), I often wonder if they are adopted.

But wait, this only child has more siblings. My stepfather, Ken Burrows, a goodly divorce lawyer who married my mom, had a stepdaughter from a previous marriage. She lives in Arizona. She is the first person I have ever met who lives in Arizona. She also has curly hair and brown eyes. We look remarkably dissimilar.

Though both of us do enjoy packaged foods, diet soda, and the comic styling of Dave Barry—but then again, who doesn't?

Then came my three adolescent uncles, Rusty, Gusty, and Lusty. Let me just say one thing about this and then not say anything about this ever again. Okay, maybe not, but whatever. If you marry someone in his eighties—early or late eighties—you just don't marry them for anything but the sex. Yes, Stepgranny was a nymphomaniac or necrophiliac.

Did I mention the shock of the century—that Stepgranny got all the money? Well, she did. I chronicle my many and complicated feelings (greed, annoyance, greed, annoyance, greed) about this in my second book, a not-quite-fictional memoir, *Girl (Maladjusted)*, a comic tour de force or something. So Stepgranny got all the money and I got all the memories. Ah, the memories—but back to being an only. I think it is best that we now cut to one of my favorite memories: Mom and me in a shrink's office. It was not our first joint session, not our second joint session, not our third joint session, not our fourth joint session, not our fifth joint session. It was in fact the forty-fifth time that Mommy and I had shared the comforting ministrations of a shrink.

And this also wasn't the first time that each of us had brought her own shrink. One shrink to one Jong: It was an amazing ratio, the kind one might find at Silver Hill or Hazelden (ah, Hazelden, thanks for the memories).

"I ruined my daughter's life. I'll admit it. It's true."

"Finally." I was fifteen, and I had figured out what the problem was. The problem, as I saw it, was my mother. She was evil and bad and everything was pretty much her fault.

Mom's shrink intervened. "I caution you not to speak in these absolutes."

"Yo, Dr. Mel Practice. The woman was just making some real progress."

Dr. Practice didn't like me very much. Perhaps Mom had poisoned her mind against me, or perhaps she was just repressing or sublimating the trail of drug dealers and lunatics that invaded my parents' Upper East Side co-op on a daily basis. "Look, your mother has become such a good mother, she takes you on book tours with her, to Europe. She introduced you to Helmut Newton. She's taken you to the Saatchis' house."

My shrink grimaced. "Let's focus."

"No, I can face facts. I ruined my daughter's life by not having any more children."

"What?" I looked at Mom.

"If you had some siblings you wouldn't be such a spoiled brat."

"Thanks."

"Ladies . . ." My shrink tried to get our attention.

"In fact, now is the perfect time to tell you this. Your stepfather and I are adopting a Chinese baby. Yes, we're adopting a Chinese baby!"

"See! This is what I'm talking about!!! Dr. Practice? This isn't really fair. She's making threats."

Mom paused. "Oh, that's not a threat, that's a promise."

I looked at Mom. "So you're going to adopt a Chinese baby?"

"Yes! Then you can learn about sharing!"

The shrinks had been here before with us—everyone remembered the Chilean baby fiasco of 1993.

Mom looked at Dr. Practice, who was egging her on from the sidelines. "And you can start by sharing your inheritance."

"Gee, thanks, Mom."

"Well, at least a Chinese baby will be grateful. After all that time in China."

"That's so racist. You don't know anything about China."

"I know a Chinese baby would be grateful."

"Mom, that is the dumbest thing I've ever heard. China could be a great place. The Chinese baby might be mad at you for taking her out of China."

"Not when we give her your room."

"What?"

"Oh, she'll be happy, plenty happy, in your room. I'm sure she won't even miss China."

"You don't know that China isn't fabulous."

"I do know that a Chinese baby would appreciate and love us in a way you certainly don't. Your problem is that you've never suffered. I had two sisters. I know suffering. We shared a room. You have never had to share. You've always gotten everything you've ever wanted and that's why you're so intolerable."

Of course, she wasn't wrong about me being spoiled, but the Chinese baby loving her back into happiness was a dubious plan. Of course, that said, I knew she'd take a shot at it.

I also knew that Mommy lived in a seven-room co-op, which meant that one of us (the Chinese baby or I) was going to end up in the library. And as much as I liked CliffsNotes, I did not want to end up in the library.

"Mom, this is the most ridiculous thing I've ever heard. I'm your little baby. Did you know that I love you more than anything in the entire world? I'm your little baby. I'm your little—"

Dr. Practice interrupted. "I would encourage you, Molly, not to go too far into the pathetic begging."

"But pathetic begging is my thing."

The other doctor agreed; pathetic begging was my thing.

Dr. Practice chimed in, "Molly, you have to understand, your mother is famous and brilliant, and she is one of the founders of feminism."

I hated Dr. Practice. Dr. Practice was herself famous and that made it just so much more annoying that she was so snowed by Mom. "So?"

"So I think that a Chinese baby might just be the thing that could change your life, Molly."

"To what?" I gawked.

"A baby might get you to forgive your childhood," Dr. Practice ventured.

"Forgive my childhood for what? Mom, this is completely nuts. Is it just me or has the world gone cuckoo for Cocoa Puffs?"

Dr. Practice looked at me. "You have a lot of denial, don't you?"

"Clearly not enough," I said.

And so I left that therapy session with my mother, and I grew up. Mom fired Alger Hiss, the squirrel-murdering caretaker, and instead hired one who wanted to murder me (long story). Mom and Ken never did adopt a Chilean baby, nor did they adopt a Chinese baby, nor did they adopt an Iraqi baby. But they did get a very annoying dog that they love much more than they ever loved me. Her name is Belinda Barkowitz and I hate hate hate her.

Sometimes my mother (who neither cooks nor eats) cooks three-course dinners for her. This really annoys me. Sometimes my mother cuddles with Belinda and talks to Belinda about her feelings. Sometimes my mother spends hours paging though Belinda's baby book crying and talking about how much she loves her puppy.

And do you know what the best part of all of this (i.e., the only child except for the dog thing) is? The best part is that Mom wanted to name me Belinda but was unable to due to my father's resistance. So the greatest joy is that Mommy instead was able to recycle the name and use it for her second daughter, her little baby, her slobbering standard poodle, and that makes me very very very happy.

And so I will end this essay as I end so much of my work, by comparing myself to a black standard poodle with a Jew fro. Yes, celebrity children and celebrity pets often find themselves in a face-to-face fight for column inches on Page Six.

And in the final analysis there will be winners and losers in the fight for only-child survival, and then there will be the one act you should never follow—A DOG ACT.

Imaginary Enemies

Sarah Towers

B Y T H E T I M E I was eight, I was ready to settle for a chimp. My campaign to convince my parents to give me a sibling had gone absolutely nowhere. For as long as I could remember, Baby Brother or Baby Sister had been at the top of every Christmas list I'd ever made; it was what I chanted in my head when I blew out birthday candles or caught my digital clock reading 11:11; it was what I pretended was true when I slept over at Navah Perlman's apartment and heard her baby brother, Rami, crying down the hall. Navah would roll over and put her pillow over her head, but I, lying next to her, and under her celestial-white frilly canopy, would open my eyes to the dark and long to go to him. What if he were mine to hold? What if this baby, with his blue eyes and strawberry blond hair (not quite as light as my own duck blond, but certainly far closer to mine than to Navah's dark brown) were my relation, my companion, my protection against the shameful tininess of my own family?

"A chimp?" My father appeared to be thinking it over. He was sitting, as usual, in his orange velvet wing chair in the living room, a book on his lap and a plate of four sugar cookies on the book-heaped table next to him. I thought I might have a shot. My father adored monkeys of all kinds. On Saturdays, when he wasn't working on a review or his next book, he'd take me to the Central Park Zoo to watch the chimps and gorillas. As a kid growing up in Richmond, Virginia, he'd had a high-strung old capuchin named Jocko whom my grandfather had rescued from a low-rent traveling show, and who lived in a pen at the bottom of the garden. They'd had to get rid of Jocko when one day he sunk his incisors down to the bone of my father's index finger, though that hadn't dimmed my father's affection for monkeys in the slightest. To the contrary: I think he felt guilty about Jocko's removal—he'd been told, ominously, that Jocko had gone to a better place.

"A chimp," I repeated. I hoisted myself onto the back of the chair, and sat with my legs dangling down over my father's left shoulder. I tapped my feet into his ribs until he gripped them still.

"Chimps are a lot of work."

"I'll do everything. You and Mom won't even know he's here."

I had it all worked out in my head. The chimp would live in my room, in a crib we'd borrow from the Perlmans. I'd be the one to change his diapers, feed him bananas, and, best of all, carry him around the apartment with his legs locked around my waist, and his arms hugging my neck. I'd pick him up and put him down. He'd stretch out his arms to be held and hop in place whenever I came into a room. I'd close my eyes and let him press his soft hairy palms against my cheeks.

My father was silent. He wasn't saying yes, but he wasn't saying no, either. From where I was sitting, I couldn't see his face. He might have been considering my argument or, as was too often the case, simply staring off into some spot in the middle distance that I could never see. His second novel was called *The Monkey Watcher*. I had no idea what it was about, but I'd often studied the author photo, and knew that it had been taken on one of the park benches outside the Central Park Zoo. The date on the photo was 1964, two years before he met my mother. He *did* love monkeys— as much, I figured, as he loved my mother and me.

"Please?" I said, prodding his rib slightly with my heel.

"Well," he said at last, "we'll see." He opened his book. He was done with this conversation. Ready to go back. "Okay, hop off, now."

I didn't move. Instead, I picked up his hand and began to squeeze the loose flesh of his knuckles up into ridges. I loved the skin on my father's hands: It was sun-spotted and wrinkly and good for molding.

"Sarah. Please. Off."

Reluctantly I dropped his hand and slid off the side of the chair.

"Why don't you go see what Mom's doing."

"Mom's on the phone with Janet."

"Well . . ."

Even though he was looking right at me, I could feel his eyes being pulled helplessly back to the page, as though the printed lines were a delicious undertow. My father was forever slipping beneath the surface, leaving whoever was in the room with him all alone.

I sighed and headed out of the living room. No point in going to my mother; her bedroom would be thick with cigarette smoke, and she'd have the phone pressed hard against her ear. I went into the kitchen and looked at the clock. It was 7:00 p.m. An hour and a half until bedtime. I wandered out and down the back hall to my bedroom and sat in the middle of my bed. I listened for my parents but couldn't hear them. I felt my chest begin to tighten with dread. An hour and a half. The thief and his wife were getting ready, they were making their plans to break into our apartment on the thirteenth floor, murder my parents, and steal me.

They would come once my parents had kissed me good night and shut the door. They'd been coming for months now, skulking around the shadows of my room, sniffing out the apartment, studying the habits of three people who always seemed to be in three different rooms. They were going to get me any night now and there was absolutely nothing I could do.

MOST OF THE time these days, I don't dwell consciously on being an only child. I go about my work and life without the constant longing that I remember plaguing me as a kid. I have a number of very close friends, people I've known, in some cases, for more than twenty years. I have a husband and a stepdaughter and in three and a half months I will give birth to my first child, a boy. In the middle of the night I hold my drum-tight belly and feel my son's kicking. I am astounded by the sensation, by the internal pats and swishes. There is someone else here with me. I am not alone.

But I know, too, that this baby won't save me from loneliness. He won't save me from the plain fact that when both parents are gone, there will be no one but me left in my original family. He will be many things to me, but never a companion who shares my deepest past, a witness to my childhood, someone who can, say, confirm that my mother once warned that I'd get blood poisoning if I pricked my thumb on a rose thorn—that I didn't just dream that up. This baby's presence will not blot out the bitter voice that can still pop up in my head when I watch my friends or husband bantering easily with their siblings, the voice that wants to know, Why not me? I loathe that voice, drenched as it is with envy and self-pity. It cuts me off from people, roadblocks conversation and connection, and returns me, fittingly, to the very state of ancient loneliness I'm always trying to get away from. Whenever I shake it off, I feel like a fever has broken. I feel less shame.

And shame was certainly what I felt about my family's size when I was growing up. Three was an unlucky number, an awkward number, always two to one. We were a hopping, three-legged mutt, instead of a graceful, bounding retriever. There could be oppressive silences with only three people in an apartment. Honest hustle and bustle was hard to come by. Rambunctiousness, with its tripping, unabashed syllables, was not a word associated with our home. My father didn't roughhouse; my mother didn't tickle me until I screamed.

There was also, for me, the nagging question of why only three. Why not four?

"You're perfect, you're all we want," my mother told me on many occasions, but I wasn't so sure. Maybe there was something shameful about me. Other parents—like the Perlmans, for example—loved their kids so much they had five of them. Mrs. Perlman, in fact, would talk to me and Navah about how much she adored the sensation of being pregnant, or of how breast-feeding, nourishing another human being, was the most important and satisfying job in the world. If Mr. Perlman happened to be around, she'd lay a long romantic kiss on his mouth—in front of us! Both my parents were older than my friends' parents (my father was a good fifteen years older, and also came from a prim Southern background) and seemed to be embarrassed by public displays of affection. At least in front of me, they never went beyond a quick peck. I didn't know the word "sexy" back then, but I could recognize electric—and wish it charged the rooms of our apartment as well.

ONE OF THE things that *did* unfailingly electrify the air in our apartment was when I got sick—and I was always getting sick.

"She should go to the doctor," my mother said one evening, around the time of the chimp campaign. I had come home that afternoon with a scratchy throat and clammy forehead, and she stood over me now, flicking her wrist to shake down a thermometer. She stared at the tiny lines, then popped it in my mouth. "It might be strep."

My father, already irritated that he'd been called away from his book and orange chair, stood by my bedside and muttered, "It's not strep. Christ, Pat, don't overreact."

At the word "overreact," my mother overreacted. She had trained as an actress in her early twenties, and she knew how to do a fight scene, with eyes narrowed, and voice steadily rising. *My father was oblivious! He was a minimizer! He was willing to let me lie there while a virus that could* blind *me, for God's sake, embedded itself in my throat!*

I scrunched myself farther down under the covers. I was with my father: I didn't want to be sick again and have to stay home the next day. That fall I'd already missed our class reenactment of the signing of the Declaration of Independence, Navah's birthday party, and our class trip to the Cloisters.

Then again, I was with my mother. I didn't want to go blind. There was a blind homeless woman who begged near our apartment, on the corner of Eighty-seventh and Broadway. There was spit in the corners of her mouth, and her eyeballs were a smeary white. I imagined that the original color had been bleached out by the disease.

An awful thought occurred to me: What if they got a divorce?

I turned over on my side. My tongue felt heavy and dead resting on the cool glass tube of the thermometer. I didn't want to think about what would happen if I bit it and poisonous balls of mercury rolled down my throat. My mother had warned me about mercury, too. At the very least, the mercury would surely burn holes in my voice and I'd never talk again.

I thought about Navah and wondered what she and her big cozy family were doing right then. Probably all watching TV together and eating bowlfuls of ice cream. I rolled over to my other side. I tried to shut out the sound of my parents' rising voices. They were locked in together and I couldn't break through.

An even worse thought came to me, and I felt my chest tighten against it: What if I was trapped sick in this bed for the rest of my life?

THE THIEF IS painfully skinny, with sharp elbows and a bobbing Adam's apple. His eyes are pale blue and watery and, like my father, he often blows his nose on a damp handkerchief that he keeps in his back pocket—and which I am sure he is going to gag me with. He is a sniveling yes-man, this thief: Whatever his wife says, he does. She, on the other hand, listens to no one—certainly not to my own pleas for mercy. Her mouth moves fast, and her teeth, which are stained a tobacco yellow, seem ready to bite any-thing that gets in her way. She is, I imagine, planning to use those teeth to chew me up.

Some nights are worse than others. I lie in bed with my stuffed animals arranged in a useless barricade around me and watch the shadows on the ceiling. My parents have, at my request, left my door open. I strain to hear them elsewhere in the apartment but can't. They're probably already dead, lying slumped over in their chairs, their necks slit. A floorboard creaks. Then another one. I curl my-self up like a shrimp. They are coming. I can hear the thief breath-ing through his mouth, I can smell his wife's moldy perfume. I tell myself not to panic, to stay calm, but it is too late—I'm panick-ing, my throat is on fire, my fever must be spiking, and in another instant they'll be opening my door and leaning over me with their horrible liver breath hot on my face, and before I know it, before I can stop myself, I'm screaming "MOM! DAD! *HELLLLLP!*"

My mother appears in my doorway a few moments later. My re-lief at seeing her is enormous. I am saved. She is alive. Nothing terrible, nothing too murderous has happened.

Her mouth, though, is turned down, and she is shaking her head. She looks sad. "Oh, sweetie." She sighs.

SOMETIMES I SECRETLY liked being sick. My mother, as my father would say, had an "imagination of disaster," and sickness—my sickness—definitely put her on a kind of thrilling alert. To-gether, in sickness, we had purpose. My father would be gone for most of the day, and my mother and I would exist in the dim, hu-midified quiet of my bedroom. She'd bring in the tiny black-and-white portable so I could watch reruns of *I Love Lucy* and *Bewitched*. The day would be punctuated by small meals—cinnamon toast, strawberry Jell-O, macaroni and cheese—and fever checks. My mother's hand or lips were constantly on my forehead, sensing for heat, and I'd raise my face up, as though to kiss her.

When I did have strep throat (five times over that fall and winter when I was eight) and was too miserable to sit up or watch TV, she'd pull a rocking chair right by my bed and read to me. When the illness was less severe—she'd always insist over my father's protests that I stay home for a full day after any kind of fever—she might bring me magazines to cut out into collages or shoe boxes to make little mouse apartments with, or, if I was really stir-crazy, let me get out of bed and wander around our book-filled apartment. Often, I'd take the blanket from my bed and use it to make a fort in my father's orange chair. Sitting under the blanket, with a flashlight and a couple of stuffed animals, time would slow and become pocked with fascinating nooks and crannies. Entire crusades could be undertaken in the space of an afternoon. It was as though magic—the magic and wish-granting I'd read about in my favorite books—really did exist: For those wonderfully lost and alone moments, at least, that which was broken could be fixed, that which was hurt could be soothed, that which was desired could be found.

On days like that, I didn't mind being an only child; on days like that the thief and his wife left me alone.

ONE AFTERNOON, TOWARD the end of that long winter, when I'd been out sick for four days and my parents had seemed to battle nonstop about the extent of my illness, I found a copy of a novel a friend of the family had written and inscribed, "To Bob and Pat and the baby within."

I was thunderstruck. The date was 1976, which meant I would have been six, and so the author clearly wasn't talking about my mother carrying me. Who had she been pregnant with? And what had happened? My first reaction was one of tremendous, flushing, relief: Our situation wasn't as shameful as I thought; my parents had at least *tried* to have another baby. It meant that if they had tried after me, they might yet try again. It meant that for a brief period, while that baby was in my mother's belly, I wasn't the only child in this family, I wasn't the only one in danger of being left an orphan if anything happened to them, and, most important, I wouldn't be absolutely alone if they did die.

I didn't tell either of my parents about my discovery. I kept it to myself, hoarded it like chocolate. Once I was well and back at school, I'd come home and take the book down from the shelf, flip it open a few pages, and stare at the loopy writing, at the phrase "baby within." I imagined this baby, safe and warm, tucked up inside my mother's beautiful belly. I didn't think about its sex, just the pure babyness of this baby, and how it would be able to hear my mother's heartbeat and bump up against her soft pink insides. Looking back, I see how much I must have wanted to be that baby myself—and that may partly explain why I put off asking my mother for the full story on how the baby had died, and resisted thinking about it myself. Without the full story and the tragic ending, I could float along in my imagination, me and the baby, the baby and me, the two of us forever entwined.

But that spring, a few weeks before I turned nine, I did ask. My mother smiled—a little sadly, I thought—after I presented her with my evidence. "Sweetie," she said, "that's not about a real baby. John was talking about how all of us have a character inside, a kind of innocent, made-up part of ourselves."

"You're lying," I told her.

She shook her head. She pointed out that the title of the book was *Babble,* and that the first chapter, which I had neglected to read, was about a Baby who shows up one day, sits on the narrator's lap, and tells him stories about Life. The Baby was like the imagination; it was metaphorical, she said—whatever that meant.

For a second, I felt a block of fury in my stomach so gripping, so murderous, I thought I might knock my mother over.

Before the tears could come, I was off, running toward my bedroom. I crawled under my bed, even though come nighttime that's where the thief and his wife often waited for me. But daytime was a different matter; there was nothing under there except tufts of dust, and I lay flat on the floor for a long time.

It couldn't be that my parents were all I had, that they were everything in the world to me, and still I was separated from them; still I was in danger of being left alone.

I pressed my cheek against the cool wood. I felt like I might die of disappointment. It was all becoming clear. There was no baby. There was never going to be one.

FOR A FEW days I remember walking around and feeling as though I had no insides, as though if someone were to cut me open they'd just find dead, empty space. I turned down two invitations to play at Navah's house. I didn't want to see her; I didn't want to see Rami. I told my father I didn't feel like going to the zoo that Saturday. Chimps were dumb, I announced. I didn't want one anyway.

The furniture in the apartment took on a strange, unfamiliar sheen. I noticed cracks in the ceiling in the kitchen. I found dried olive pits in a side table in the living room. I tried to imagine what would happen to everything in the apartment if my parents suddenly died. There was so much stuff stuffed into every closet and drawer: cards and coasters and necklace beads and Italian coins and grapefruit spoons and mystery keys and checkbook stubs and enamel boxes and fans and newspaper clippings and my old baby clothes—it was too much. All of it made me feel helpless and inconsequential, and I didn't want any of it.

I took to holding my breath, to timing myself with my stopwatch to see how long I could go. I'd do it during any spare moment—after social-studies class, before dinner, in my bath. I imagined I was an athlete in training, told myself I'd better beat my record *or else*. And every day I could go longer: forty-five seconds, forty-nine, fifty-two. The tight rush in my head blanked my thoughts, and it felt dizzyingly good to be so close to fainting, like standing with a toe over a precipice. But the explosive exhale was even better. I'd lean panting against a wall or over the side of my tub, red-faced and wet-lipped, tingling with the swift, suddenly oxygenated current of my blood.

There was no baby, I told myself. No baby.

For a while, every night seemed to be worse than the one before. I could hear the thief running his fingers around the perimeter of my room, leaving a slug trail of germy spit. His wife had supernatural vision and had taken to staring through the sheets, through my nightgown to my naked body.

He wanted to infect me; she wanted my body. I couldn't bear it. Who were these monsters? What made them think they owned me? And why couldn't they just leave me alone?

IT IS AFTER dinner. My father is in his orange chair, a book on his lap. My mother is in the bedroom, watching *Upstairs, Downstairs*. The apartment feels big and hushed, but tonight I don't mind as much as usual. I have some cooking to do.

I grab a mixing bowl, an egg beater, and a wooden spoon from the kitchen, and bring them back to my bathroom. I pull out ingredients from my medicine cabinet: calamine lotion, baby aspirin, Kaopectate, hydrogen peroxide, bacitracin, and the nasty oatmeal bath mix my mother used when I had the chicken pox. I dump it all in the bowl, add two cups of water, and stir until the mixture turns a nice brownish-green color. I add a sprinkling of baby powder, flicking my wrist just as I have seen my father do with the salt shaker, before placing the bowl on the radiator to cook.

Later, I lie in bed with the covers pulled up to my chin and try not to look at the shadows on the ceiling. The poison is under my bed. I wait and listen. Nothing. Maybe they aren't coming tonight. Maybe they found out about my plan. I clench my toes against this idea, against the unfairness of it, now that I am ready. Hours and hours seem to pass.

But then—is that a sniff? A muffled cough? The sounds grow louder and unmistakable. I shut my eyes tight and pretend to be asleep. I can hear them whispering, making their terrible plans. I hold my breath.

Suddenly, my room erupts in total chaos. They have fallen into the poison and their skin is coming off in giant curls, like wood shavings. I open my eyes in time to see the thief's wife dancing and shrieking around my room, before she rushes to the window and jumps out. I hear her descending scream, the thump of her landing dead on the sidewalk. The thief, meanwhile, runs into the bathroom to try and wash off the poison, but it is too late, it is shrinking him, and in two seconds he is sucked down the tub drain.

I flick on my bedside lamp, my hands shaking. I can't believe it but it's true: They're gone. I am absolutely alone. For a moment, I don't know what to do, and wonder, crazily, if I will miss them: They have, after all, kept me company every night. But then a strange, oddly powerful feeling starts to tickle up me, like a flush: They are gone, but I am still here. I have saved my own day.

I turn off the lamp and lie back and look around my room, which even in the dimness suddenly seems much bigger. Light from the apartments across the courtyard pools in the center of the room, and I can easily make out the edges of the bookcase, the desk, the rocking chair. I start to hold my breath—it's become habit by now—but then stop; my chest doesn't feel as empty as usual. I close my eyes instead. The sheets feel good against my body, cool as glass. My pillow has just the right amount of downy lumps. From behind my closed eyelids, I picture my room again. It's really not a bad room—four strong walls, two windows, a high ceiling. It has possibility. It's where I'll be for the rest of my life. It will have to do.

AIR ONLY

TED ROSE

M Y PARENTS DON'T see eye-to-eye about much, but
they agree that my birth heralded the end of their marriage. I was barely out of the crib when my mother
moved halfway across the state. My father responded by driving
halfway across the country. By the time I could walk, I faced a
major geographic challenge. My so-called family unit spanned
more than a thousand miles. I was one small boy without a brother
or a sister, armed with only my golden hair and my sweet fat cheeks,
chasing one outsize goal. I wanted to make the world right again,
and I had no other choice than to pursue what I considered my secret plan: I would bring my parents back together.

In order to see both of my parents regularly, I flew on airplanes
regularly. When the airline people decided that as a five-year-old
I could fly without supervision, I flew alone. I liked it. I liked eating the overcooked steak off a plastic tray while watching a bad
movie; I liked listening to the pilots chatting confidently with the

air-traffic controllers; but most of all I liked the attention. Being a child on an airplane alone in the seventies was a big deal. When I flew, the crew decorated me with a pair of gold wings, the same ones worn by the guys in the cockpit. Pilot's wings. These days, unaccompanied minors are given Day-Glo paper wristbands like you might get in a lousy club, but I was treated like a minor celebrity, a pint-size Lindbergh. My seatmates always quizzed me and admired my spunk. I grew to understand that I was good at riding airplanes, and I liked being good at things. I liked the idea of being special. I liked it mostly because I did not like the alternative. If I wasn't special, then I would have to be ordinary. Most people presumably had families waiting for them somewhere: a wife or a husband, a brother or a sister, even a pair of parents. But I had no family down on the ground, just two people who lived very far apart. If I wasn't special for flying alone, I secretly understood, then I was just plain alone.

I SPENT THE school year with my mother, living in a three-story white gingerbread house with green shutters that sat on a prominent corner of the Wesleyan University campus in Middletown, Connecticut. The house, just down the hill from the school's observatory, used to belong to an astronomy professor. I peeked out from my window up on the second floor and watched the tours go by. The upperclassmen walked backward past our house while addressing the ever-present group of curious high-school students and parents. They bragged about the well-known English professor who lived in this very house. I looked into the eyes of the kids and saw envy. Who wouldn't want to live in this house? I asked myself. Well, me.

My mother was a charmer, don't get me wrong. Under her leadership our house became a premier destination on the central Connecticut literary landscape. She hosted dinner parties that stretched late into the night. In the morning she closed her study door, and in the afternoon she emerged with reviews completed, chapters written, and classes prepared. I reluctantly concluded that none of this had anything to do with me. I spent most of my time at the house next door dreaming up skits with my friend and his sister in the attic. When I got home, I stayed in my room and watched television: cartoons first thing in the morning and sitcoms late into the night. I had my mission, of course—I would bring my parents back together—but in the meantime, like any ace pilot between sorties, I spent a good chunk of time cooling my heels.

I anticipated travel days. Those were the best. Those were the days when I saw both my mother and my father and it was almost like we were one family again. I shared this tortured logic with anyone who would listen. I clung to it with determination, as if repeating it enough times with enough conviction might actually make it true. I didn't care that my parents barely spoke to each other, and that when they did it was to coordinate my trips. If I could make my story fly in this world, I could do anything. I could easily bring my parents back together.

When I started traveling alone, the airline let my mother bring me on the plane. She had her maternal moments, and this was always one of them. She put me in my seat and fussed about for a while before reluctantly hugging me and leaving. I put on the pilot's wings and remembered my mission: have fun. I scoured the seat pocket in front of me for candy. I collected as many decks of playing cards as I could by propositioning different stewardesses.

When my dinner tray arrived, I snagged the pepper package next to my chicken breast and tore it open. Once I watched Road Runner trick Wile E. Coyote into sniffing pepper, which produced a terrific sneeze. I decided to replicate the experiment. I opened the package and poured the black contents into my pudgy palm. I held my hand against my nose and breathed in. My toddler body was rocked by a powerful quake. I opened my eyes. The seat back in front of me was covered with red dots. I looked down and saw my grilled chicken had red flecks, too. I held up my hands and took in a horrific sight. Everything was covered with my blood. I never imagined that a cartoon gag could produce such a real-world punch line, but this wonder gave way to fear. If an ace pilot makes a mistake, he's no longer an ace. I was not ready to give up being an ace. I went into full cover-up mode. I cleaned up the mess and acted as if nothing had happened.

Early on, I assumed my plan's success hinged on winning over my father. He was the one who'd left my home state, after all, the one who'd chosen the West over my company. It stood to reason that if I could persuade him to change his mind, everything would revert to normal.

My father looked like a hippie, with his beard and his banjo, but he was a little older than the longhairs and a lot more conservative. He lived in Woodstock during the summer of '69, but he cleared out of town before the festival arrived. He entered academia at a time when university jobs were a safe bet, but I happened to arrive on the scene at the most precarious moment in his career. He toiled away as an assistant professor in the Ivy League, where a tenure position glittered in the distance like an unapproachable oasis. When his marriage to my mother went south, he grabbed the only certain offer on the table, a tenured job in Illinois. He later recalled the day he drove to the Midwest, suddenly without his family, headed for a second-tier school in a state he'd never given a second thought to, as the worst day of his entire life.

My father lived in a bland ranch house on a street lined with bland ranch houses that dead-ended in a cornfield. When I arrived I always felt like an honored guest. He dropped everything when I came to town. My father would take me to the museum or to the zoo. At night, he'd set up the telescope in the backyard and we'd stare at Mars and the Andromeda galaxy. I liked the attention, naturally, but it never took long before I started to feel an acute sense of absence. I missed my house. I missed my mother. I missed my friends most of all. I wanted to play with them, not this middle-aged bachelor. I couldn't let him see that, of course. He needed to see me happy, because that was the only way he might end this ridiculous experiment and come home. So when the visit began to drag, I professed cheerfulness and secretly looked ahead. Other children anticipated birthdays and Santa Claus; I fantasized about my next trip across the country.

On one flight back to my mother, I sat next to a blond Swedish woman who expressed a great deal of interest in my life. "Yes," I told her, "I'm flying alone." "Yes," I told her, "I like flying alone. I like these days when I get to see both my parents." I smiled big and then pretended to drop off to sleep, which was the only way I had figured out how to end conversations politely. A few minutes passed, and that's when it happened. Her hand moved across the top of my scalp and then down the back of my neck. She made this journey once, and then again and again. Once again, I was caught off guard. I didn't have a plan for this contingency. This little petting episode quickly mushroomed into a full-blown political crisis in my brain. Why was this woman touching my head? She was either molesting me or seducing me, I decided, or both, and I needed to fashion a response, but I had no response to these fears. While the woman gently stroked my head, probably wishing me good things, I nervously played dead.

While my father was the reluctant exile, my mother and her career thrived. But the woman had a temper. She'd get furious waiting in line at the supermarket or fume about the package that never arrived in the mail. I was never the direct target of her anger, but that came to be beside the point. I still tiptoed around the house. What if she did decide to turn the wrath toward me? The stakes were simply too high. I secretly counted the days until I once again took flight.

I REMEMBER THE trip when it all changed. I was in the front seat of my mother's station wagon on the way to the airport. I was seven years old. It was a warm, muggy day, the beginning of summer, and I was leaving all of my friends behind. Of course, I told myself, I was thrilled. I told my mother I was thrilled, too. She put on a Creedence Clearwater Revival tape and we sang along on the way to the airport. Then the traffic thickened. We were still far away, but we slowed down considerably. There must have been an accident somewhere ahead, though I couldn't see it. My mother grew quiet and stared ahead. I could feel her getting nervous. I didn't know that she was thinking about my father waiting at the other airport. I didn't know how she was dreading the moment when he would call her, irate that I missed the plane. All I knew was that her mood was darkening and that the traffic was getting worse. I had my work cut out for me. I did what I had trained my-self to do: I smiled. I stoked a light conversation. "Isn't that a strange color for a car?" I asked her breezily. She didn't respond. I would have juggled pinecones to convince her that everything was going to be just fine, but I was out of my league. I could tell myself how special I was, I could feed off the adoration of everyone around me and fantasize about a reality in which I had the power to change history like Superman flying around the world backward, but I had about as much of a chance reversing this woman's mood as I had of making the traffic disappear. Still, I couldn't keep myself from trying.

The car stopped moving altogether. We were trapped in a mo-tionless river. My mother couldn't restrain herself any longer. She exploded. She pounded her fists on the steering wheel. She screamed and she cried. She was my mother and then she was no longer my mother. She was a little girl. She was a little girl who was not getting what she wanted. I sat next to her, cringing. I squeezed myself tight and prayed I might disappear. I shut my eyes and saw awful things. I saw a plane crashing into the ground and flames all around me.

WHEN I WAS in my thirties, my mother decided to move out of the gingerbread house and I went back to gather my stuff. She would be away, and I was intrigued by the prospect of spending time in the old house alone. When siblings aren't around to help you reconstruct a childhood, those physical trips down memory lane become even more important. I remembered the house as a castle, but when I returned, it felt small and besieged. The once-quaint English garden in the back had gone feral. Rhododendron pressed against three sides of the structure, while on the fourth, the house next door had ballooned to three times its original size and now served as the college admissions building. I sat out on the porch as one of the tours appeared, led by a startlingly young docent walking backward. She told the crowd that my house was home to the college's book-publishing imprint, which was not true. Her mistake left me exchanging awkward stares with her tour group. I no longer saw envy in those eyes; I projected bewilderment. *What is a grown man doing sitting on the porch of a book publisher?*

I climbed upstairs into the attic, the place where I spent my teenage years. I roasted in the summer and froze in the winter, but I loved the attic because it was my own. Or used to be. In the last decade, my room had been turned into an extended storage area for my mother. Old boxes of her manuscripts lay on the carpet, while my stuff was piled in the closet. I found the *ElfQuest* comic books I had collected when I was twelve years old. I had started buying them because my friends liked the series, but I had never felt the urge to read them on my own, deciding instead that they were a good investment. I unearthed old journals and notebooks and read through my entries. I wrote in these private spaces the same way I collected the comic books, dutifully, imbued with a resigned faith that by jotting down these notes somehow they would be of use later on. But the impulse was always halfhearted. Thoughts often ended abruptly and notebooks inevitably petered out. The writing felt rushed, as if the writer always had somewhere else he needed to go.

Within two hours, I had finished packing. Every material possession from my childhood lay in one of three cardboard boxes or in the Dumpster in the driveway. I treaded lightly as a child and left little behind. Sitting cross-legged on the worn carpet, I realized that although stuffing my childhood with television and travel and fantasies had not managed to bring my parents back together, I had accomplished another, albeit unintentional, mission. I had successfully prevented myself from experiencing my own life.

THAT AFTERNOON OF my mother's meltdown, the traffic cleared, my mother recovered, and I made my plane. I continued to shuttle back and forth between my parents for years. I'd like to report that once I'd lived through my mother's tantrum and finally comprehended the folly of my mission, I chucked the tactics that supported the mission as well, but I did not. I kept flying.

As I entered adulthood, my flying only increased. I no longer constrained myself to bouncing between my parents. I began to move from job to job, girl to girl. I stayed in one city for years, but I always talked about leaving it. Then one day I did leave. I bought a car, packed it tight, and started bouncing across the country until I had no address at all. For a few weeks I drove through the mountains without any destination whatsoever. Every day I would wake up and drive a few hundred miles. I didn't care much where I ended up as long as it was very far from where I had started. I was completely floating through the air until eventually, inevitably, I began to drift back to the ground.

I settled in Colorado, where I find the geography soothing. This place is not only in the middle of the country; it also straddles the Great Plains and the Rocky Mountains. It is also a place where, aside from a few friends, I am alone. My preferred activity these days isn't flying; it's gardening. I've always felt the urge to work land, but until recently I never had a plot to work. The house I rented came with a garden overgrown with weeds. Because I arrived in the fall, most planting was out of the question. I decided my modest task would be to prepare the soil to lay fallow over the winter. I appreciated the simple task of pulling weeds, of returning to the same patch of land again and again and witnessing the cumulative effects of my labor. I still feel the urge to abandon the garden, to fly off somewhere else, but sometimes I don't feel that urge. Sometimes I am grateful just to be in my garden and spend a few minutes kneeling in the dirt.

THE HOTLINE

ALISSA QUART

SANTA WAS NEAR Alaska. At least that's what the voice on the other end of the phone line said. "Ho, ho, ho." Sleigh bells rang in the background. "The elves have done a great job this year. We are flying over Antarctica. Ho, ho, ho." Ten minutes passed. Santa had a new message. "Mrs. Claus says hello." And then: "Hold on, Rudolph!" Followed by: "You have been good and Santa will be in your neighborhood very soon." Then the clattering of hooves. "Ho, ho, ho."

The year was 1980. I was eight. It was the night before Christmas Eve and I was alone. I was always alone in spirit, although most of the time I had someone to watch over me, a babysitter in her twenties like the bohemian one with thinning hair, a long scarf, and a manic elfin aura who explained to me the real story behind my favorite song, "Lucy in the Sky with Diamonds." Or maybe I was with the historian's daughter, who laughed at me for reading in the dark. Or maybe the heavyset judo enthusiast, who pinned me down on the living-room floor in one sweaty, exciting episode. Reaching further back, there was the one who wore tinted pink octagonal glasses, who took me into her communal college housing in 1976 and stuck a button for what I believe was a Weathermen-like group on my little jacket. And then there was the one who locked me in the bathroom for hours.

I was at the dead center of an absolute New York only childhood. Franny and Zooey had nothing on me. I was growing up godless, in a home of chaos and kilim rugs. My father prevented me from attending Hebrew school, telling me, "No child of mine will believe in God!" He was a post-1968 Abraham, sacrificing his daughter not to God, but to the absence of God.

In rebellion against my father, a professor who celebrated comedic nihilism and for whom every day was a living anniversary of the comedian Lenny Bruce's death, I was one corny child. I liked fantasy, sentiment, schmaltz, phony ritual, cardboard-cutout cheer, gumdrops, rhinestone earrings, Holly Hobbie dolls, carols, and cartoons of animals, the things that in my father's opinion were "false consciousness." Alongside these corny things was a distinctly seventies creation, the Santa Claus Hotline. I had called it ten times already. I would call it ten times or maybe twenty times more that night. It was my introduction to corruption, repetition, and diversion.

The Santa Claus Hotline was my consolation, a solution to my weird existence and the absence of ritual. It came to me in a flash, appearing in an advertisement right after an ad for steak knives that cost $19.99 and one for *John Denver's Greatest Hits*. At seven o'clock, I was on my eleventh Hotline call. "Ho, ho, ho. We are over Canada now!" it said. Again, there was the clatter of hooves.

This telephone Santa was a conduit to gingerbread houses and human houses containing two young parents and two young children. Indeed, the phone calls and the sterile chipper messages were an unlikely source of salvation, forming a metaphoric chain, like a folding bridge, to another world. That other world could have been Narnia or it could have been Wonderland. Whatever it was, it was in reverse of the typical alternative universe. It was a place with other children my own size, sugary soft drinks, and sportswear, skis, and tennis rackets. There was someone my own size to beat me up and in the background, the vibrato of unashamedly childish voices. It was a world *more* normal than the one I grew up in.

THAT CHRISTMAS WAS like all my Christmases as an only child. They were piled high with "the special snow of oblivion" (Nabokov). But it wasn't just Christmas. On all the days of my life, I was in the keep of my ancient-seeming parents. There was my mother blotting her lipstick, the popping poppy red of the later 1940s, into a pattern language of SWAK marks on napkins in restaurants, and my father, with his sage brutality, like an outtake of a lesser Philip Roth short story.

Their Home of the Only Child was no home to Childhood. Barred from the premises were mac and cheese, Disneyland, Santa. But at seven, I still held out the hope of having my childhood corrected. I wanted another sibling. So my mother said she might have one.

In my mind, this infant would arise immaculately. According to distorted sexual curiosity, I answered my own question of how babies were made with a homemade myth: Babies derived from an orange pill that a mother swallows. I asked my mother when she might swallow another. My mother was disturbed that her own flesh and blood was so pagan. She explained with earnest liberalism how babies were really made. I listened and decided I had lost my innocence, preferring my more *Valley of the Dolls* fantasies about big bright orange pills.

When might my mother get in "a family way"? I asked. She wouldn't answer; she just told me that I was so special they stopped at just one. Maybe one day there'd be another. (In later life I would act as she did. I wouldn't dissemble exactly, but I'd make promises I couldn't keep, a labored passivity.) Being the only child gave me a distinct feeling that I was nearly unborn. That feeling matched my father's joking claim that he never wanted a child at all. The phrase I thought of regarding being an only child then was *"One is almost none."*

On Christmas Eve 1980, I was thinking I had nothing to believe in, which meant I had everything to believe in. That anything could be real, including Santa on the phone, gum drops, and God, and that the space of negation was a mere two degrees removed from the fullness of faith. I checked in with the Hotline: "Have you been good? I think you have been good. Ho, ho, ho," it said. I saw, in my mind's eye, a collage of unstoppable, meaningless Christian happiness: Santa, in his red polyester suit, with his air of all-encompassing rescue, the glass ornaments that dangle from trees, the miniature wreaths that look as if they are covered in sugar powder, the carolers with their beet-red faces and mufflers and migrant Midwest cheer startling the cheerless as they pass them on city street corners.

On the phone, Santa clearly had promises to keep. He made me a promise of presence and arrival. He made a promise of a normalcy that would, clearly, never be realized. "We are in Newfoundland," the Hotline said. "Be ready for a surprise in your stocking." I knew better and went to sleep, pressing my head as close as possible to the wall.

I WENT THROUGH the years, Christmas-free, enthralled by sentimentality. It made sense then that television became my favorite found object. For a long time, I didn't venture to turn on the television by myself. But then when I was six, I fiddled with the old Panasonic dial and . . . life itself. My parents had lied to me again, I realized, this time about the wonders that lay within that deep box. They had neglected to mention channels playing all day and all night. I understood that television channels were the allies of children in their war to slay their loneliness or boredom. I watched the garish sitcoms: *I Love Lucy,* for one, which even then I understood as distressing. After all, what's so funny about a lousy marriage? I watched the cartoons, all sharp geometries and sugar cereal colors. I watched the "grown-up" car-chase shows in which every man looked like Burt Reynolds's cousin, their black mustaches communicating things to me and other viewers that we would never consciously understand. I feared the women on variety shows with bare midriffs, stringy hair, and tans the color of pumpkins. I watched the older soap-opera actresses and liked that their false eyelashes were so long that fake snow fell in them and stuck there during the tragic love scenes. Upon discovering TV, I was angry to learn that I had spent six years unaware of this whole world of gushing idiocy. I projected myself into the soap-opera towns as if I was simply the latest resident, the sad-eyed ingenue.

These places were so wonderfully artificial and so occupied by people who needed people, knew people, and hated people. My favorite aspects of the forbidden television channels were, of course, the nuclear families, blankly opening cardboard presents, their eager fingers undoing the gifts wrapped in reflective red-and-green paper. The television presents mounted beside the blond-headed torsos of the television people. I suspected there was nothing under the wrapping—but still, the children on television got these false presents by the dozen. And why not? It was a Studio City Christmas Day and everything was going to be all right.

Beyond television, I had lots of other nonhuman friends. I possessed imaginary girlfriends with the names of cartoon sexpots like Lana, Lorna, and Lina. The Robert Moses of imaginary cities, I built towns on my bedroom floor—expanding, secular, civic crèches that were almost unbearably peopled, as if inventing the many would correct my super-stark onliness. I had some other nonhuman friends that I recall were rather inanimate. They were the tiny hopscotch game of brown and sienna on the linoleum kitchen floor and the stars that could be drawn out of the patterns on white wicker kitchen cabinets. There were the books and more books. I read at least one a day. My favorite books featured orphans, and I saw myself in Oliver and Pip, Nell and Jane Eyre, girls and boys making themselves small, folding themselves into other families' lives, trying not to try anyone's patience. These girls and boys could well be ejected from their newfound brood at any time so they knew full well they couldn't bother anyone. I, like them, needed other people's families and other people's houses, my face pressed to the metaphoric glass. I was offered the cast-off boots, the extra blueberry pancake, yesterday's jokes, and yesterday's family cross-words, but as an observer, I was not entitled to the hearty, bovine stances that blood family walked around in. A lack of ease was my default setting. I was always poised on the edge of chairs, the corners of rooms, the smallest space, so no one would find me asking too much.

Other people's families served junk food, which was my manna. Their Christmas pine trees were beguilingly and seductively placed in their parlors. I loved that the true center of their homes was the entertainment center—even the term "entertainment center" was joyously trashy yet comfortable at the same time, connoting a Las Vegas of the living room. I also envied the kids who got proper children's gifts at holidays: toy cars, toy stoves, brightly hued sweatshirts. In short, gifts that helped children become more childlike and less like strange little people. I, though, didn't get gifts for any holiday. Instead, my father gave me recommendations of books to read and a lecture on the decadence of Christmas. Sometimes, there was an accompanying lecture on the middle-class smugness of *Jewish* holidays in America, their deracinated piety. I was so happy the one year I got chocolate Easter eggs that I hid them under my bed for a year. When I was ten, I think I insisted on lighting the Hanukkah candles myself, but I was discouraged when I realized I didn't know any of the prayers. I recognized that Santa would never arrive bearing either tangerines or coal, no matter what the Disneyesque hound dog on TV that had goaded me to call a mechanical Santa twenty times had said. Likewise, no sibling would arrive to end my daily life as my father's apprentice—walking as he walked, talking as he talked, trying to think as he did, trying to predict his changes in mood. I was fast becoming a strange little person and no one was stopping it.

Then I discovered the impossible. I discovered how to not be an only child. I became a girlfriend. I was thirteen. I was never *not* someone's girlfriend again. The boyfriends had teeming families, and I stayed with the boys and their families from adolescence on. Night after night I soaked up their propriety. Christmas and other holidays filled in the considerable gaps in feeling in these families. Holidays elicited strangers and relatives. In the living rooms, I found cousins, exchange students, diplomats, all eating Christmas cake and Stilton cheese, playing games, sounding noisemakers. There were so many people that I was lost in the crowd, and happy for it. One boyfriend was twice my size and nearly twice my age. He had two mad sisters and his father had died when he was a newborn, but he also had a chosen family, headed by the Holy Father. At Mass, his eyes were wet with tears. He knew Latin. He sang in a high tenor. He never read a book that had been taken out of the library after 1940, which meant that he read Vedic books and the works of the lesser saints. He was plump and rather plain, but I thought he was incredible.

For the most part, each boyfriend's family was a clown car of intimacies. I grew attached to his sister and her girlfriend, his haughty mother, his infinitely girlish aunt, his self-controlled father, his yukking-it-up New Age brother. And then he went away, often because I sent him away. I liked the phrase "object permanence," but I saw that I had a knack for avoiding it. That made sense, though. I longed for objects to be permanent, but not the boys in particular. The object I wished for was a family tree, the aunts and the brothers, the tooth fairies, centaurs, gods and goddesses, and the Santas, half men, half cathode ray, all bearing the present of Americana.

IN TIME, THE Hotline was right. Santa did arrive.

In 1980, I had tried to find him by phone and discovered the joys of corrupt repetition instead. Thereafter, I resigned myself to his absence. But in 2004, twenty-four years after the Hotline, at a Christmas party in Beverly Hills, Santa finally appeared. He was, however, rather different from the man the animatronic voices once promised me.

Sure, Beverly Hills Santa was clad in a red polyester suit. He was ensconced in padding. He had the white nylon whiskers hiding his face. He arrived at a party composed of an upper class swathed in velveteen and lamé, abutted by numerous children, framed by a huge tree of pink and yellow lights, and the finest piano on which the Christmas songs might be played.

When Santa arrived, these guests applauded. They laughed as their many children sat on the man in red's lap, in this year's performance of a play these people had been putting on for fifty years.

I, too, sat on Santa's lap. But I was thirty-two and "Santa" was my boyfriend. In real life, my boyfriend was gray and urbane, taking in everything and giving little back. Then, after eight o'clock, he turned into the secret comedian of the living room. I prized him most for his barely visible qualities—dry wit, a puerile streak. Twelve years my senior, he came from a huge family. He was always in the world—every object on the walls of his apartment derived from a country with a timeline different from our own.

•   •   •

THAT CHRISTMAS, this boyfriend played Santa despite the fact that he was Jewish by birth. On Christmas Eve 2004, he was masquerading as both Christian and playfully sentimental. It was as if someone had tried to cue the tinny baritone of the long-ago Santa Claus Hotline. "Ho ho ho," the Hotline might have said. "Slow down, Rudolph. We are near the palm trees. We are landing on the roof. Santa is in . . . Beverly Hills." Seated on the Santa simulacrum's lap, my black hair mingled with his synthetic white beard. Innuendo and camp prevailed. Who would have thought?

Still, had you told me when I was a child that this is how one catapults oneself momentarily out of aloneness—through Christmas in quotations—I might not have been surprised. Since age eight, twenty-four years have schooled me in how one's lot in life can be altered but not really changed, although change is all we desire and what we also require. I am not the only one who knows this. It is evidenced in the way in which we wonder, Have I changed or been changed or changed another? There are those grand poems and cabaret songs that exhort transformation when we all know full well the impossibility of a person's fundamental change. "You know what I was/ You see what I am: Change me, change me!" is how Randall Jarrell concludes "The Woman at the Washington Zoo." Rilke writes, "There's not one spot that doesn't see you. You must change your life." Nina Simone sings, in an exquisite cover of the Comden-Green classic "Just in Time," "Change me! Change me! Change me once again!"

As an only child, I learned early, however, that basic transformation was impossible—I would always be the single child, watching the shadows the bookshelves made on the ceiling from reflected streetlights, a gloomy lattice of Culture—and that special solitude could not be changed. It could, however, be forgotten. It was just that by thirty-two, I had come to know that substitutions *were all there were*. Sitting in the lap of a Santa who was also a boyfriend was a transformation of a sort: by doing so, childish longings had become kittenish adult kitsch.

But no funny alchemy can alter the human story that is also my story: that we are all one, which is almost none, and that the only child is simply the most exaggerated version of all of us, growing up, alone.

BECOMING AN ONLY CHILD

ELIZABETH DEVITA-RAEBURN

I WASN'T BORN an only child, I became one.

I had a brother. Ted was the elder by three and a half years. He'd been there as far back as I could remember. My compass, my map. What he did, I did, or aspired to. What he liked, I liked, or learned to. He was nowhere near as enthusiastic about me, which didn't at all impair my slavish attempts to gain his approval. At age five, I gave up *Sesame Street* and professed my loyalty to his favorite show, *Star Trek*. Spock was no Oscar the Grouch, but you do what you have to do. Getting to lie on my stomach in front of the TV, elbow to elbow with my brother, was worth the trade-off. Bit by bit, year by year, I assembled the pieces of myself—what I wore, what I thought, what I ate, how I played—mindful of my brother's critical eye. And then, one morning when I was six, I woke up and he wasn't there.

It was late September, still warm enough for us to wear shorts. One night during dinner, my mother glanced down at my brother's legs and said, "Will you look at that; he has more bruises." We all peered down. The bruises weren't of the faint polka-dot variety that we tended to accumulate going about our daily lives. They were big and colorful, like spilled pots of paint under the skin. My father, an oncologist, had seen his share of them—at work. He looked down at the blue blackness spreading across my brother's thighs and knew he had a blood disorder. He just didn't know which one. He didn't let on, though. He said something about bringing Ted to the office after dinner, just to check him out, and we all went back to our plates.

They kept Ted at the hospital overnight. By morning, they had a diagnosis: aplastic anemia, a rare immune disorder (you're more likely to get struck by lightning) in which the pulpy marrow at the center of bones, where white and red blood cells and platelets are manufactured, stops cold. It's an insidious disease. On the surface, the symptoms are benign—pallor, fatigue, bruising, shortness of breath. Nothing, with the exception of the bruising, that you wouldn't attribute to feeling a little run down. And who, with the exception of people like my father, gives more than a passing thought to bruises? Meanwhile, the immune system is silently vanishing.

By the time he was diagnosed, Ted's immune system was almost gone. And there was no treatment, only the stopgap of transfusions to temporarily replace the missing cells. Plan A was to keep Ted at home, let him try to lead a normal life, and bring him to the hospital for periodic transfusions. Thus, after spending a night in the hospital, my brother came home with a bloody gauze patch on his hip where they'd used a needle and a hammer to extract marrow from the bone, and the treasures with which they'd had to bribe him—paper packets of sterile gauze, tongue depressors, and plastic syringes (without needles), which we spread out on the living-room floor like Halloween candy.

But that wasn't the end of it. One night a week later, Ted woke up with a high fever. My parents panicked. They rushed him to the hospital, where they executed Plan B. The doctors put Ted in a sterile, ten-by-ten-foot "bubble" room—in actuality a regular hospital room divided in half by a clear plastic curtain. The far half was kept sterile by an elaborate air filter built into the wall. The half near the door was as germ-ridden as the rest of the world. The only link between the two was a doorway-size opening in the plastic, near one wall, through which Ted's food and medicine would be passed. On the floor, a red strip of tape continued the curtain's line to the wall, the words "Do Not Enter" spelled out in red tape in front of it. The ventilation system on Ted's side created a steady, thrumming breeze that kept germs on the outside.

The rooms had been created only recently, by a colleague of my father's, for cancer patients whose immune systems had been knocked out by high doses of chemotherapy. But in those people, the immune system usually bounced back. In Ted's case, that wasn't presumed. The idea was mostly to keep him safe from bacteria and viruses and whatever else might prey on him. Meanwhile, they'd keep up with the transfusions and hope that his bone marrow would spontaneously sputter back to life. Or that a cure would come. I knew nothing of this at the time. I was only six. In Plan A mode, I suppose, my parents had hoped they wouldn't have much to explain. And I was asleep when Ted woke up with the fever and Plan B went into effect. My parents called a neighbor to sit in the house while I slept, unaware of the drama that had unfolded in the bedroom next to mine.

TED'S ENTRANCE INTO the bubble room left me in a gray zone, unsure of whether I really was a sibling anymore. My life certainly didn't resemble that of any of the other brothers and sisters I knew. Every day, I got up and went to school, my mother went to the hospital to see my brother, and my father went to work. At three o'clock, I came home from school and my mother came back from the hospital. At six, we ate dinner. At seven, we all went to the hospital, sitting in the nonsterile half of his room, which, Goldilocks style, had three seats—a yellow vinyl stuffed chair, which my father monopolized, a hardback chair with minimal cushioning, which was my mother's, and a squeaky rolling footstool, which was mine. My father adopted his customary pose, head buried in medical journals, yellow highlighter in hand, while my mother and I watched my brother's TV through the blur of the plastic curtain. Nothing so different from at home. But it wasn't anything like home.

Once, my brother and I had spent the majority of our time together, separate from my parents—watching TV, playing in the backyard, playing on the block with the other kids. Now our relationship took place almost entirely before our parents' eyes. Getting into trouble together, or even questionable territory, wasn't an option. No more partner in crime. Gone were the days when my brother would give me a follow-me look and we'd sidle away to explore a box of matches or a forbidden street. Gone were the days when we could confer about the behavior of our parents. Gone were the scary stories he told me, out of our mother's earshot. And gone was the physicality of our relationship—the punching, hitting, slapping, and hand-holding crossing the street. We looked at each other now through a curtain, a ten-year-old and a six-year-old, with no idea how to conduct a relationship neither of us had ever given much thought to. Our life, together, had fallen away like so many leaves on a tree.

At home I was alone, outnumbered, now, by adults who'd always left it to the two of us to take care of keeping up the child-world in the house. Without my foil, an eerie quiet crept in. I no longer had to share the pink-and-black tiled bathroom at the end of the hall. I could walk into my brother's room without knocking anytime I pleased, without fear of reprisal. I could monopolize the TV. I no longer had to sit in the backseat of my mother's station wagon, where my mother had exiled both of us rather than listen to us fight over the passenger side. Now I climbed into the front seat, without question. I got to choose all the sugary cereals that went into the pantry. All the prizes they contained were mine. The dog played only with me. These were all things I had pined for when my brother was an immovable presence. But once he had proved himself movable—something that had never crossed my mind as a possibility—it didn't feel good.

I did not feel deliciously entitled. I did not bask in my largesse. Instead, I felt bereft, as if someone had walked away from me in the middle of the most intense conversation of my life. I recognized the approximate sensation years later, in college, when I was one of only two people to stay in the dorm over a holiday. It wasn't that I was always interacting with the other girls, or my roommate. Or even that I liked living in such a crowd. But I was aware of their presence, and their presence signified a social structure that defined the microcosm of a world we lived in. When they were gone, that world disappeared, and I felt lost and disoriented. That's how it was without Ted in the house. I no longer knew how to be. The board games started to collect dust—there was no one to play them with. Instead, I turned to a more solitary pursuit—books.

My brother's physical removal from my immediate life extended to the way I was with others. Somehow, it had stripped something from me, something I'd thought was internal. At the dinner table, I didn't know how to make the patter, which my brother had helped create, happen. My parents and I sat listening to one another eat. I, whom my mother had always described as the gregarious one, became shy, serious, and introverted. And at six, I was new to elementary school. Before my brother had gotten sick, he'd escorted me the two and a half blocks from our house to my classroom and picked me up afterward, a daily ritual that had made me feel safe and protected. Without him, I felt like a turtle without its shell. And it showed. I quickly attracted two bullies—one who haunted me during recess, the other who knocked into me every day as I traversed the path to and from school.

EIGHT AND A half years passed with Ted in the bubble room. I got used to the way things were. The hospital had become an extension of my world, as unremarkable as going to the mall. I'd become used to spending my free time there, and seeing Ted through plastic. We had adapted to our situation. We had an elaborate number of facial expressions and eye rolls we used to express our thoughts about the outrageous behavior of our parents. We could silently agree to bait my mother into her trademark sigh, and just as silently smirk at each other over our success. Instead of punching and slapping, we'd learned to insult each other, verbally. Who ever ran out of comebacks first, lost. Our repertoire of shared TV shows had grown from *Star Trek* to include old movies, PBS series, Dirty Harry movies, and Jacques Cousteau specials. And we had learned to call each other on the telephone, when I was at home. It was our only means of talking privately.

But I was still stuck in the gray zone. Did it count if your brother didn't live in the same house with you? I feared not. The house was still too quiet. As was our dinner table. I preferred to hang out at the houses of friends with lots of siblings. While they'd spend all their time trying to find ways to avoid their brothers and sisters, I was always looking for the opposite—the raucous breakfast table, the group slouches around the TV, the spontaneous wrestling matches. I was always on the lookout for extra siblings, standbys. On the rare times that I saw my cousins—we didn't travel because we couldn't leave Ted—I spent as much time as possible perched in the lap of the boy cousin almost exactly Ted's age. And I had long since started referring to my godparents' three sons as my "god-brothers," steadfastly refusing to acknowledge that my claim didn't extend that far. I was getting by. We were getting by. Making do. I thought, someday, that my brother would come home.

It was the transfusions, not the disease, that did him in, according to his medical records, which I read only recently. Iron is a trace element in the blood. But with all the transfusions, Ted's blood had built up more than a trace over the years, and the excess had damaged his heart. One night in mid-May 1980, when I was fourteen and on an exchange trip to Scotland, Ted collapsed. Tests showed that his heart was flabby and enlarged, failing. He survived for two weeks, during which time I returned from Scotland—no one had told me what had happened while I was away—and got to see him, wan and laid out flat in his room, IVs in both his hands and feet.

On May 27, a night I had decided to stay late with my parents in the waiting room at the hospital, a code rang out over the intercom, summoning the defibrillator cart to Ted's room. This had happened before, in the previous two weeks. My brother's heart was having a hard time keeping a regular beat. Thus far, the paddles, or, to his doctor's amazement, a biofeedback trick he'd taught himself, had always brought it right again. This is how I assumed it would be again. Ted always won. Who knew that better than I, the one who'd always had to lose to him at Monopoly? Even behind a curtain, he was invincible. He had, for instance, long since started doing his own finger sticks, and he terrorized the roving phlebotomists and IV starters on the ward, instructing them on which veins they were allowed—or not allowed—to use on any given day.

But this time was different. My father, when he heard the code, said, "This is it." I didn't understand. Neither of my parents had discussed the possibility of Ted's death. Ever. Our sentences frequently contained the phrase "when Ted gets out." And despite the fact that it had been eight years, it never occurred to me that Ted could really disappear. It seemed like we could go on like we had forever. Or that he would get out. One or the other. That he would not, in some way, be in my life, never occurred to me. And then he died. No brother anywhere. And my transition from a kind of sibling to an only child was complete. I stood next to my father on the other side of the curtain while my mother gowned up, went in the room, and propped up Ted's head. And I watched, in utter shock, as the lines on the heart monitor grew flat.

· · ·

We went on, and like many families who have lost a child, dealt with it badly. Finding the subject of Ted too painful, we erased him. We rarely mentioned him. My father refused even to say his name. My mother made his room into an office for my father. Any mention of Ted, even pictures of him, became taboo. Too painful. His birthday, and the day of his death, passed every year without comment. When people asked me if I had brothers or sisters—a loathsome question I could smell coming a mile away—I always said no. And it was true. I didn't. Any obvious trace of Ted, save for an obscure stone in a remote cemetery, had been entirely obliterated. We had officially become a family of three.

That my brother had left indelible footprints on my psyche, that he was not so easily erased, was not obvious to me. It took me well into adulthood to begin to explore what his life and death had meant to me, and then only with the help of my brother's medical records, which told the story my parents still refuse to tell. Until I read them, my understanding of what had happened remained as I'd known it at age six. And I still didn't know what I was: sibling or only child? My mind was at war on that point. The records recounted the entire story—the blood counts, the pallor, the bruises, my brother's apprehension the night he went into the bubble room, the evolution of Plan B, the full eight-and-a-half-year struggle, and, to my horror, the results of his autopsy.

I was not mentioned in the records, other than as a possible bone-marrow donor. But I could trace the sad progression to my life as an only child, next to his. And it was only then that the quirky conundrum of my identity started to become apparent to me: I was both a sibling and an only child. Wired one way, living the other. Like a transsexual. Like a transsexual who didn't know she was a transsexual. It became even clearer with the recent odd coincidence of being asked to speak, along with some other bereft siblings, to a class of soon-to-be social workers about the nature of the loss. And then, that same week, to attend a meeting of only children who had been tapped to contribute essays for this book.

In the first group, we talked about our siblings, about how our brothers and sisters had defined us, about the hole they'd left in their wake. Our grief, and the way that so few had seen it. In the second, we spoke, wistfully, about what it had been like to grow up alone. We talked of the quietness in the house, growing up in an adult world, the overinvestment of two parents in the sole child in the house—both in childhood and adulthood. We talked about wishing for a companion—and how different that might have made things. We talked about envying the people who had siblings, and trying to acquire them, through our friends. We talked of having to manage our parents, and learning to navigate life, alone. My life, during Plan B and afterward, very much resembled theirs. In short, I belonged to both groups.

And I realized that with little exception—a couple of people had really *liked* being only children—both groups were essentially talking about loss, and loss of the same kind. They had just experienced it in different ways. One group was examining the hole left in their lives, the other what might have been added. Neither was entirely fathomable. How can you gauge the depth with which the people we love and live with leave their traces in you—after the fact, or hypothetically? That's what we're all searching for, those of us wistful onlies, in these essays, in one way or another. We're asking how our childhoods, or adulthoods, *we,* would have been different had they been some other way. And there is no way to know. We have only the lives we've lived to work with.

I am satisfied, if not happy, with the explanation I've arrived at—I am a sibling who has lived most of her life as an only child. Hearing the shared stories of other onlies confirmed that for me. I have a leg in both worlds. I have learned to adjust. I have acquired friends who are like sisters, and a husband who teases me like a brother. I now say, "I had a brother," when people ask me if I have brothers or sisters. I keep a picture of the family of four we once were at my bedside. And I still have the cheap, faux-wood table we were all sitting at, eating dinner, the night my mother remarked upon the bruises on my brother's thighs. My husband uses it as a desk. My mother keeps telling me to get rid of it, that it's worthless. But I can't. Because it's not.

II

WE ARE...

FAMILY

Significant Others and Friends

Triangulation: A Love Story

Deborah Siegel

I. Three

*I*N A FAMILY *of three, one is always left out. Rarely, if ever, is that someone me. Instead, I am the apex of the triangle, the pinnacle, the point that makes our triumvirate cohere. Or so I imagine things to be.*

I don't always get my way, and, at nine years old, I take it personally when the office door snaps shut, signaling the start of a session. Free to enter without a key but not allowed upstairs, the intimate strangers known as the Patients are my imaginary siblings, competing for my parents' time. They come because they're broken. My parents, I know, can fix them. I know this because my parents try to fix me, sometimes, too.

My parents are magicians, capable of keeping women from walking into lakes and men from leaving their wives. Sometimes whole families come to see them. Sometimes there's screaming. More often, crying. My room lies directly above the office, and at times, after the door closes, I climb the stairs, go into my room, and jump hard, up and down, on my bedroom floor. Momentarily locked out of the intimacy that is my birthright, I am not inclined to share my parents with the strangers who leave their shoes on top of my Tretorns in the basket in the front hall.

Only I must.

At age ten, I dance around the office in between patients trying to get my father's attention. Finger rising slowly up to pursed lips mouthing "Shhhh," my father casually wishes me away. "I'll be with you in a moment, Deb," he says, covering the speaker part of the phone with the palm of his hand. He's on the phone with a patient, and I'm supposed to understand. A good girl, I usually comply. Except sometimes I don't. Those times, my mother intervenes. "Your daughter needs you," she'll mouth in a hiss, a whispered code I'm not supposed to understand. But, of course, I do. When it comes to my mother, I read minds and lips.

Even when she speaks in tongues, I understand her. My mother and I share a language of sideways glances, intuitions, invisible words. Unlike my father, who draws a limit, she's a master at anticipating my desire.

I've heard it said that mothering a child is like watching your heart walk around outside your chest. To my mother, for whom there is only me, I am heart, spleen, and marrow. She is quick to take me at my word. If I'm anxious, she'll find a solution before I know what's wrong. Rarely, if ever, am I allowed to feel uncomfortable in my skin, perhaps because it is her own. More often than not, I relish being the object of such undiluted attention. But sometimes, when the focus becomes too acute, I feel like I might catch fire.

When that happens, I run down the driveway, down the street, around the corner to my best friend Busy's house. Busy is one of six siblings, and in Busy's house, I'm happily anonymous. They call me Daughter Number Five there, and I wear my number with pride. At Busy's, we play Trolls or backgammon, or watch All My Children, and later we'll smoke pot and drink beer. But mostly we hang out with the sisters and my "other mother," whom I call Aunt Peggy, in the library, a lovingly cluttered room with well-worn couches where family photographs (always, the six of them) spill from overstuffed bookshelves. Inevitably, the phone rings. "Is Debbie over there?" My mother's voice follows me, anxious echo courtesy of Ma Bell. Aunt Peggy and I shoot each other knowing glances. I negotiate a reasonable return time—sometimes I think my mother merely misses me—and the girls and I go back to our game.

Around this time, I have a recurring nightmare: My mother and I are lying on parallel gurneys in an operating room, having mandatory surgery to exchange our eyes. Later, I have a dream where I feel beautiful, and the minute the sensation of pure joy washes over me, my mother disappears.

In real life, she never disappears.

My mother is ever-present, and essential to my survival. She makes life easy. She takes me shopping, and out for "ladies' lunches," and drives me anywhere I want to go. As long as my mother is around, I know I will never be hungry, lonely, or cold. I will never stay longer than I want to at a friend's house, or be forced to stick it out at summer camp when it's no longer fun. I will never be the last one picked up from school, or the kid who packs her own school lunch. But nor will I do what other kids my age do easily. When I get my license, rarely will I drive alone. And it won't be until senior year in college that I make airplane reservations myself.

Were there more of me, I wonder, would my mother worry less, or more? In sixth grade, my parents consider adopting a baby, after batteries of infertility treatments have failed. I write about it, breathlessly, in my spiral-bound journal for English class. I'd make a great big sister! Sharing Trolls and Twinkies comes naturally to me—how else does an only child get others to play along? Sharing parents, however, is something *else, and I have a hard time imagining it, though I'm willing to try. As it turns out, I don't have to, because in the end they decide not to adopt. Who knows, my father later explains to me, what psychological baggage somebody else's child might arrive with already. Daughter and son in one, I remain an only by default. It's a designation I come to wear with pride.*

"I feel married a bit to both of you," I report to my father one day when I'm twelve. I'm beginning to experiment with independence, and I shuttle, chameleon-like, between allegiances. My parents' roles solidify: She (mothersistertwin) defends me from discomfort, and he (father-mentorfriend) from suffocation. Depending on the day and the mood, I belong to him, to her, but rarely to myself. I'm far too fond of them both to rebel.

We go everywhere together, and I relish our family vacations. Often, we'll rent a rustic cabin in Wisconsin, or later, a small house on Cape Cod. One summer, my parents amble out onto the ocean floor at low tide. Terrified of stepping on a jellyfish, I hold back, and freeze. It's not the fear of pain that frightens me but rather the gelatinous danger I can sense but cannot see. Turning back for me, my father lifts me high into the air. Riding off on the shoulders of a giant, I breathe easy, immune from invisible things that sting, and unaware, even, of the undertow.

As I enter my teens, I am dainty but tough, and together my father and I conquer the physical world. His ready sidekick, I hunger for adventure. He teaches me to sail, to garden, to control a fifty-five-pound dog on a choke collar, and to embrace a challenge head-on.

On the eve of my fourteenth birthday, my father drags me out of the house during one of those great electrical storms that roll in over Lake Michigan and straight, it seems, into our backyard. Flashes of lightning curl around us, offering declarative sentiments—dangerous and charged.

The two of us stand there, awestruck, drenched not by rain, which has yet to come, but by the giddiness of being out in a storm. Neither of us seems to care that my mother stands on the opposite side of the glass, begging us to come indoors. Later that year, when my father and I ski together down steep mountains in Wyoming during a blizzard, yodeling fearlessly at the top of our lungs, my mother cries at the bottom of the hill, convinced that we—her everything—have been lost to the storm.

My father buffers me, but I am keenly aware that my mother's fierce, singular love is double-edged. I know this because it's a source of contention between my parents, the cause of some of their more memorable fights.

Like the time she helps me cook up a lie—"We'll say Grandma had a heart attack and you had to come home"—to help me get out of a camp job I don't like the summer before eleventh grade. In reality, I'm exhausted after a draining first session and in need of a rest. But the way we handle it, with the two of us taking my complaints so seriously despite my father's protests, turns me into a wuss. Would an older sibling the next cabin over have intervened, siding, perhaps, with my father and equalizing the coalition formed by my mother and me?

"If you keep letting her out of things, she'll never learn," my father protests, an exasperated yet firm voice of reason. But it's too late. My mother is determined to keep me safe from the world. And I'm torn. I know my father is right, but I like playing Lois Lane to my mother's Superman. When he tucks me into bed that night I come home from camp, my father looks at me with sad, cowlike eyes and says, "Your mother, she worries. You and I know better. You're not going to break." But I'm not so sure. I sleep, and, upon waking, decide to return to camp. Other times, I lazily play along, giving in. Only years later will I recognize the disabling luxury of being rescued so completely.

For the moment, the arrangement feels just fine.

But at age sixteen, I feel crowded, and I write my mother a letter—a plea for privacy and a break from intrusion. We cry together, and she tucks the letter in the drawer of her nightstand, to be read over and over again. Meanwhile, I start spending more time with my girlfriends, who have by now acquired boyfriends, and dream about the day my familial threesome will, through marriage, become four.

In college I begin to shed my parents, but reluctantly. I fall in love. I read Pride and Prejudice *and* The Awakening, *and when I think about my future wedding, I imagine only the exchange—parents for husband. It's a poignant transfer, one full of happy emotion, and, as I walk down the aisle my face is awash in joyful tears. The distant groom is faceless— he has yet really to appear—but there is a face propelling the emotion, and it's my father's. (Freudians, revel.)*

In the reverie, I'm walking down the aisle on the arms of both parents. As we approach the chuppah, we stop. I turn and kiss my mother, then my father, good-bye, then step forward to meet my faceless groom alone. My tears flow openly, uncontrollably. The moment is a suspended farewell to childhood, the sacred trio, the intimate tribe, and I am overwhelmed.

In the dream, I never imagine what comes next. I take the first step forward, then suddenly, I am awake.

II. Two

I met him at the Underground, a cozy, brick-walled joint that had recently changed owners. I had been under the impression that the place was a coffee bar, but now it served only booze. I was twenty minutes late and this, I later learned, made A. angry, but at the time he didn't let on. When I first saw him, he was perched on a bar stool in an overstuffed parka zipped up to his chin. I thought he was the bouncer, his expectant glance carding me at the door.

We peeled off our winter layers and settled into a booth. There was something both boyish and bearlike about him, and I found myself compelled. An accomplished academic, world-celebrated and heavily recruited, he hungered for intimacy, affection, attention. His eyes said, Paddington-like, *"Please notice this bear."*

That evening, as we exchanged stories and pedigrees under the soft scrutiny of candlelight, I knew that this was one bear who wouldn't let me push him around. Previous boyfriends had been loving, nurturing creatures who caved too easily, I often feared, to this only child's demands. Bored with calling the shots, I had grown restless in those relationships and was always the one to call them off. Now in my thirties, I sought a partner who could beat me at my game. Seven years my senior, a dazzling intellect with a wicked wit and a famished heart, A. was the challenge I had been waiting to embrace.

Our courtship was whirlwind. We were both highly mobile— I was finishing my feminist dissertation, and he was on leave, delivering talks on legal theory around the world. We took nine trips in eight months and traveled together well. Popping open my laptop on a veranda in Slovenia, I felt I had arrived. Back home in Manhattan, we'd host dinner parties for our friends, exchange drafts at West Village cafés, and dream together of our fabulous future. The night of 9/11, we threw an ad hoc dinner to honor the living; just weeks later, we traveled to New Orleans, where we got engaged. Carpe diem, we figured. Life was short, and we were two thirtysomethings grown tired of living alone.

We moved in together, merging schedules, CDs, and lives. I couldn't wait to take him home to show him more of who I had been, and who I had become. I was more than ready, or so I thought, for three to become four.

III. Four

"You're enmeshed," declared my husband-to-be, feet dangling from a stool in my parents' kitchen, when I took him home to Chicago. It was not an observation, but an accusation. I was thirty-two. "Don't you see it?" he continued. "You're their *only child*," he offered by way of explanation.

Fury filled me, and my heart began to quake. Didn't he know how many billable hours I'd spent learning to be separate? Granted, this process had been facilitated by a shrink who had been a close colleague of my parents'. But couldn't he see now that my laughing with him at my mother's constant little intrusions signified growth? Or what a coup it was that I'd stopped equating phone cord with umbilical cord and had given up the daily calls home? "Only child" implied not grown up, and adult was something I had fought tooth and nail, albeit belatedly, to become. I still struggled with some grown-up things, like finances. I was a lazy cook and never even tried to sew a button myself. But I took great pride in small-scale accomplishments that others did on automatic pilot, like renting a car and filling it up with gas.

"Did you notice how you still call Chicago 'home'?" A. continued from his perch, citing my linguistic tic as further evidence of terminal enmeshment.

"It *is* home," I retorted. "And so is New York, with you."

I was a nation divided, with inalienable allegiances to both camps.

IV. *Five*

We never became four. We became two and three instead, A. and I forming a new unit, while the old, fluctuating trio remained a forceful presence.

In part, it was my fault. I had imagined a husband as someone who'd integrate seamlessly into the tribe, a fourth who'd join my father and me in our adventures and let my mother worry about him, too. But my mother's worrying nature, over time, tried A.'s patience. And while I had imagined ski trips with husband, father, and me yodeling our way down the hill, there was an obvious conflict of interest. While A. was willing to yodel, his idea of a ski trip was the two of us socked away at a romantic hotel in the Alps. I came to see his point.

But three also never became four because A. had a habit of building protective armor around himself in the presence of anything resembling family. He had a hard time understanding that I *liked* spending time with my parents and *wanted* them to visit. In my house growing up, life had been one ongoing conversation in which I was perpetually engaged. My parents and I were still in the midst of that conversation. In A.'s family, being together had meant sitting in the same room, everyone reading the newspaper, on their own separate page. I had difficulty understanding why any time a parent—any parent—would call us at home, A. not so subtly would find a reason to disappear.

Still, I wanted desperately for my fiancé and my father to find common ground. I longed for the circle of adventure to expand, to encompass them both. "I'll never be your father's son," A. declared one day over sushi, responding to my too-obvious desire that they bond. And there it was: A husband is not a sibling. How, then, would this peculiar, hybrid being, the "son-in-law," take shape? I decided to step out of its way and find out.

Meanwhile, our whirlwind life had taken on crushing momentum. Midway through the tornado of planning a wedding and deciding where to live—post-9/11 New York or the Midwest, where we had temporarily moved for the semester—I began to lose my grip. Stuck in what was starting to feel like Stepford, I was far from all I knew, away from women like me, alone in my despair during what was supposed to be the happiest time of my life. When an agent in New York squelched my literary aspirations by turning down the book upon which I had been banking my fledgling postgraduate career, I subsequently lost my moorings and began, bit by bit, to disappear.

I became depressed.

A. had been involved with depressed women in previous relationships and hadn't handled it well. He had been strongly advised by others that, in the future, he should try to stay away from Women Who Get Depressed. It had been his mantra during our yearlong courtship, and I could intuit the rising crescendo of his anxiety now as I felt myself seduced by the psychic undertow, struggling to make it out of bed. A.'s fear of mental turbulence was palpable. Terrified I'd scare him away if I showed even remote signs of slippage, I kept mum as chaos brewed.

During an action-packed junket to explore real estate in New

York, negotiate with university deans, and meet with literary agents, I outwardly broke down. Ducking into the safe haven of Riverside Church to take a break from the maelstrom, I let myself collapse in A.'s arms and unleash the tears and thoughts I had been keeping from him. The still air and his embrace held me, and for a moment I felt reassured. Then he stiffened, pulled back, and said this: "I've told you, I don't do this well." He told me of women he knew who had gone to farms in the country when they went "crazy." All they had to do there was throw pots on a wheel. "Maybe you should consider going somewhere like that to get back to being, you know, yourself."

In his eyes, I thought, I am losing my mind. And after that, I did.

A.'s reaction to my malaise contrasted sharply with that of my parents': While soothing words were a natural extension of their lexicon (they were therapists, after all), A.'s emotional vocabulary failed him. "I'm not supposed to be with women like you," he'd repeat after that trip in a faltering attempt to explain that it pained him not to know what to do to help me.

"I'm not crazy. I'm not 'depressive.' I'm *depressed*," I'd counter, drawing on hollow-sounding therapized words in an effort to reassure us both and assuage his fear while we waited for the antidepressants to kick in. "There's a difference." But I knew it wasn't easy for him, and it broke both of our hearts. A. couldn't believe this was his life, and he'd tell me so, again and again. Neither, I wanted to tell him, could I.

I took a break and flew to Chicago. Once there, I dove straight for my parents' couch, curled up in fetal position, and declared my intention to stay. My mother held my head on her lap while my father played Bach concertos and made me fried matzo. In my mind, the struggle became epic—a choice between this and A.— and I worried now that I would choose them, and not him, if I didn't get off their couch soon.

"Relationships take work, but they shouldn't be this hard," my father said to me on a calming walk along Lake Michigan's shore, his message as loud and clear as the waves. And for perhaps the first time in my life, I actively tuned him out. This was *my* journey, my adventure, and if it were to be a misadventure, it was to be my own.

My mother couldn't release me from this existential discomfort, but, to her credit, neither did she try. At the critical moment, she had grown strong. "This, too, shall pass," she assured me as I wordlessly telegraphed to her the unyielding agony I felt. Her supersaturated love had, for the moment, found its appropriate expression. Ever the therapist's daughter, I saw that she had learned to empathize instead of project. Though I still longed for her to fix me, she had learned by now—had my father convinced her or had life?—that her second heart, the one outside her body, must learn to walk alone. Weighing the false comfort against the fear of regression, I got up, chose life, and returned to my fiancé in New York, privileging the number two and leaving three behind.

So what did I do? Reader, I married him.

Perched high above Manhattan in a borrowed penthouse overlooking the Cathedral of St. John the Divine, our married life began. I had deliberately chosen adulthood, and with it came an unbounded sense of acceptance and calm. I tried mastering my finances and fired the shrink who attended conferences with my parents. I stopped pushing the son-in-law role and started cooking us meals. I stopped calling home, stopped calling it home. I visited less often and involved my parents less in the details of my daily life. My parents didn't call me. They respected my unspoken request for distance and didn't want to intrude. We all knew tectonic plates were shifting.

Breaking up with my parents allowed me to stay with my husband, and tighter bonds grew between us when I let some of the older ones go. But even these, fresh but deep, couldn't save us in the end. For A., it turned out, much like my mother, had depended on my happiness like oxygen. When I went under, he had stopped breathing. When I resurfaced, he was furious at me for depriving him of air.

I felt my heart grow an extra chamber as I learned to forgive him for being fearful—afraid of depression, afraid for our future, and afraid, most sadly, of me. But eventually his fear overwhelmed us both. Our marriage ended the day he asked me whether I was sane enough to be a mother. I forgave him, but it was the line I never could forget. Ultimately, A. couldn't be sure he wanted to be with me. And without that certainty, I couldn't feel safe.

V. One

"A. and I are separating," I told my parents over the phone. My mother did not take this news well.

"Does A. want this, too?" she asked repeatedly, her worry transparent. But her anxiety no longer held any sway. I was elated, having rescued myself from what had come to seem like doom.

"We're with you," said my father. But I felt them with me in a different way. They had become parents of an adult only, no longer a child. And so it was that I became one.

On the cusp of finalizing our divorce, I ask myself now, was the breakup of my marriage a failure of love, or a failure of imagination? And if imagination, then whose? I had misguidedly imagined marriage as an extension of the loving triangle in which I had grown up, only a four-legged triangle is an impossible shape. I tried hard to imagine a new shape but grew exhausted by the struggle our marriage had become before that geometry could emerge.

One afternoon, A. had said to me, "I'm not going to love you unconditionally. I'm not your parents." Is only a parent's love unconditional? I wondered. And wonder still.

It is the bittersweet lament of the only child who has been loved only too well.

LAUNDRY DISTANCE

LYNN HARRIS

WHEN I WAS maybe six, my parents sat me down to tell me that I was going to have a little sister or brother. Shortly thereafter, they sat me back down to say sorry, false alarm. My mom cried, and so did I. I cried because it upset me to see other people crying—not because I was sad. I wasn't sad. A sibling? *Uh*-uh. Sharing the spotlight, my toys, my parents' attention—sharing anything, really: Sorry, that's not in my contract.

Back then, being an only child was excellent. I realize that's a little bit like a trout saying, "Water: works for me." Only childhood was, of course, all I knew. However, I did observe that my friend Kara always had to "give Danny a turn." I witnessed the masking-tape-down-the-middle-of-the-bedroom incident with Laurel and her big sister. There was the time Tamar and I arrived at her elaborate playhouse only to find it taken over ("nO gIrLs!!!") by her brother Ben and his Visigoth pals. Christina's big sister smelled. And while I admit it was great fun to torment my friend Rachel's little sister Melanie by attaching a pencil to a lazy Susan and forcing her to make a sandwich of whatever it pointed to when spun (relish, Marshmallow Fluff, Fancy Feast), I was only too happy to come home from playdates alone. Alone to a stack of library books, to a good game of Pickup Sticks with Dad—also an only, his patience knew no bounds—to my Raggedy Ann–themed spot at the center of the universe.

There were lonely days here and there, sure. Looking back, I guess it was significant that my most vivid daydreams were not about a deadly/kindly monster eating my parents and raising me on candy, but rather about all the kids from *Zoom* coming over to play with me. It also makes sense that at the earliest slumber parties, I didn't do so well. That is, I never quite made it to the slumber part. One time—and this kind of thing happened more than once—I had to ask Teresa Theriault's mom to call my parents to come get me. I said it was because I didn't feel well, but it was really because, even with my yellow stuffed bunny to protect me, I just couldn't sleep that far away—0.75 miles across a Boston suburb— from Mommy and Daddy.

At some point, right around when I began sublimating my deep love for Shaun Cassidy with a devotion to horseback riding, I decided I did want a sibling after all. An older sibling. That could be arranged, couldn't it? Don't people get older siblings all the time? Perhaps from some earlier dalliance of my father's that I wouldn't have understood till I was older? That would have been cool.

Specifically, I wanted an older brother. You know, a hot older brother who would look out for me, tousle my hair, teach me how to throw a football and how to make out, using a pillow. You know, a boyfriend.

Alas, neither was forthcoming.

For one thing, I was hideous. Until seventh grade or so, I had the same bowl cut and clunky glasses as my dad; on planes, cabin attendants called me "son." Don't even ask about my teeth. To this day, my mom insists I was "cute." Of course, she was the one who bought my dad and me matching red and blue rugby shirts. When we sat at the piano playing duets together, even Norman Rockwell would have been like, "Eeuw."

I also didn't get out much. Or if I did, I had on my person a name tag, pepper spray, water wings. With no other siblings to distract my parents, you see, I was overprotected, overscrutinized. When I was littler, I took it in stride—again: trout, water. But when I hit double digits, it started to chafe. Having Mom and Dad *on* call from wherever I was ruled; *having* to call Mom and Dad from wherever I was did not. Fast-forwarding to age fifteen or so, once I started being invited to parties involving anything other than cake and bowling (not to mention slumber), I started . . . not being allowed to go. I was permitted only if a parent was going to be in attendance—and shockingly, my word was not good enough to confirm this. One time, my mom actually *spoke to Mrs. Donovan* to get her direct assurance that she'd be there. Can you believe that?

Well, you shouldn't. Because—through a clever plot involving precise timing and sleight-of-phone—we rigged it up so that "Mrs. Donovan" was actually my friend Anna. "Oh yes, I'll certainly be there at the party, keeping an eye on the kids," Anna said. We were *golden*. Until Mom drove up to the Meades' house, saw a bunch of fifteen-year-olds tapping a keg on the porch, let us go to the party, picked us up, and let us lie all the way home about the "movies" we'd watched, then waited for us to own up to the giant lie till she could stand it no more and grounded me for all of spring break.

Even when I was in the house, my parents—especially Mom— knew exactly where I was. Not just because the house wasn't that big; there was some sort of echolocation involved. If I so much as opened the door to the attic (repository of Mom's hilarious clothes from the sixties—as opposed to my circa 1980 gauchos, which were very serious) or the basement (repository of a mildewed copy of *Looking for Mr. Goodbar*), I'd hear, from three rooms away or another floor entirely, "Don't let the cat in!" or "Do you *have* to go in there?" (And, when I came back out, "Wash your hands!") It was often very, very quiet in our house, save for the plodding basso profundo of Robert J. Lurtsema, host of *Morning Pro Musica* on WGBH public radio. Small wonder that I spent a lot of time at Anna's. She had four siblings and parents who listened to the Beach Boys and a house so big you could smoke pot even when they were home.

I did have a handful of suitors in my junior- and senior-high-school years, though the only making out we ever managed to do required causing a disruption in the space-time continuum. If the fella and I repaired to my room, the door had to be open, and reliably, some sort of vacuuming emergency, requiring Mom's immediate attention, would occur in the hallway right outside. If I went out with or over to visit Jeff, or Greg, or Paul—never mind a chastity belt, I practically had to wear an ankle bracelet. *Call when you get there, don't leave the mall, I'll be cruising the parking lot;* my mom's machinations and triangulations could have gotten the president of the United States in and out of Beirut without a scratch.

Why all the surveillance? Because, I was told, I was special.

Especially special. It was going to take an especially special boy to be good enough for me. (Greg, he was nice, not to mention deeply dedicated to learning the first few bars of every Yes song, ever, on his bass, but he was not *special*. I see this now.) Mom informed me that she knew that now was a time when hormones would start to make me feel, well, funny, but it was better not to give in to them altogether. It'd diminish me, make me seem . . . less special. It was better to play it cool.

At the time, I didn't understand what she meant at all. Whatever happened between me and Ellis Feldman under the blanket during the movie at the youth group overnight—by now, I wasn't calling my folks to take me home early—*that* made me feel special.

Going away to college was a revelation. Now, I admit that Connecticut isn't *that* far away from Massachusetts, except on foot. (If I'd applied to any college west of Northwestern, or any college with "west" in the name, even, my mother might have seen fit to infiltrate the Educational Testing Service and tamper with my SAT scores.) But still, out of sight, out of mind: My parents loosened their grip. Oh, the freedom. And oh, the *crowds!* Why, there were people *everywhere,* even in my own teeny bunk bedroom, which I happily shared with a basketball player from South Dakota with four siblings. (That thing about only children being spoiled? Apocryphal; clearly invented by a sibling with an ax to grind. Onlies are generous to a fault—I've lost so many things I've loaned—because we've never had to defend our stuff or space from anyone else.) Our suite, the whole campus, it was like Anna's house, with or without the pot; no, it was more like an exotic, noisy foreign country, one where I spoke the language and could do as I pleased.

In college, there were two big-deal boyfriends. Mom gave me

the safe-sex talk about the first one, freshman year, before we'd ever even done it! Ha-ha! In a perverse way, this made up for lots of the things I actually had done, and gotten caught for.

After college, I rented an apartment in Somerville, Massachusetts, with Juliet, my best friend from seventh grade, who'd escaped to boarding school earlier on. There, I began to see signs that the period of democracy and liberty, of arts and letters flourishing unfettered, might be coming to a close. Mom's phone calls became more frequent, her concern more profound about whether or not I had a "chicken" cutting board. College? Ivory tower. But Somerville! This was real life, complete with the myriad ways I could mess it up—and all only laundry distance from home.

In Somerville, I started freelance writing part-time, and I saw fit to get myself one of those newfangled thingamabobs called a fax machine. My mother, also a writer, got one shortly thereafter. I found this out when I received, unsolicited, a fax from her number. On it, in the same hand that had penned my name on all my lunch bags and camp clothes, was written in giant capital letters: "YOUR MOTHER IS WATCHING YOU."

And underneath was a crooked little heart with a smiley face inside. In context, it had all the effect of the grinning white-frocked doll who wakes up and stabs you in the night.

I complained—and I feared the facsimile—but let's face it: When I actually *wanted* my parents' attention, I got it. For one thing, my just-for-now office-assistant job was at MIT . . . in my father's building. It was this crazy ramshackle place that was built as a temporary barracks during the war but never torn down, full of students tinkering with solar cars but never going outside. So no, I did not bring laundry home, thank you very much. Rather, I brought it to Dad, and he brought it home. It came back clean and folded beautifully, sometimes with a side of brisket.

And as I began my writing career, my mother was more than generous with her editing services. In order to allow time for Mom to give every article her once-over, my self-imposed deadlines were a day earlier than any given magazine's. I don't think I handed in a single article between 1990 and 1995 without Mom's signing off on it.

I also called home a lot. Recipes, favors, reports of triumphs at Filene's Basement, decisions large and small. Juliet and I talked everything to death, too, of course. There was even another serious boyfriend: practical, wise, capable, the kind of guy who always has a flashlight. (I called him L.L. Bean.) Nevertheless, I went *with* him *to* things—Allman Brothers concerts, his folks' house in Maine—I didn't go *to* him *for* things. Anything big, or even medium, needed the parental imprimatur before it could happen. My folks knew it was over with Bean before he did.

At about twenty-six, I moved to Brooklyn, signing a lease—this was big—on an apartment my parents had never seen. Mom, a native New Yorker, let the cord go slack fairly willingly here; perhaps the extra loads of laundry had finally lost their charm, perhaps—given that I'd spent my childhood living out her own Fresh Air Fund fantasies of tree-climbing and farm camp—she was somehow ready for me to come full circle, back to the motherland. (My dad, born in then-rural Georgia, had always said, "You can't raise a child in the city!" My mother's position: "Where else would you raise one?")

I loved Brooklyn. I loved my apartment, I loved my roommates (two dear college friends, both guys, one gay. Sort of a P.C. *Three's*

Company). Still, New York, and my late twenties, early thirties, were also where being single started to smart. Not that there weren't boyfriends—Jewish ones, even. But I was getting to "that age." Not only were more and more friends getting married, but here and there, not often but often enough, friends' parents were starting to die.

Where will I be when that happens to me? I started to wonder. What if I have to make big life—if not death—decisions by myself? When, God forbid, one parent is grieving for him- or herself, whose job will it be to support *me*?

When I found out that my grandmother had died, I was standing in the Pantheon in Rome with my cousin Ken, watching dust glitter like daytime stars in the slanting column of light from the roof. (Ken, who was teaching in Rome at the time, is like my ninth cousin a billion times removed, cubed. I was on a trip with a friend; that day was the one day I spent with Ken.) My parents called with the news on the cell I was carrying mainly for that purpose; how fortunate—and, I thought, foreshadowing—that I happened to be with family at the very moment they told me. I figured that Ken, along with my first cousin Hillary and my other fifteenth cousin Sarah—all about my age—might forever serve as the spouse stand-in.

Because the guys I was dating, they weren't cutting it. To be fair, my tales are not tales of Dating Hell, unless you count the day I burst into tears, at the end of my single rope, when I got a flirtatious e-mail from a guy on Match.com whose lone photo involved a beer sleeve and vampire teeth, or the guy who read nothing but books about dreams and his own dream journal, or the night I walked home from a wedding—my fiftieth! I was counting!—at the Brooklyn Museum, sobbing, pumps in my hand, hem dragging on the asphalt, because the mensch who'd flirted with me all night had hopped a train for New Haven without saying good-bye. I called Mom that night from my teeny cell phone, whimpering that I was doomed to a life of listing my parents as my "emergency contact."

But the longer-term few, they were lovely: a devoted fan of my ice-hockey team, a mixer of the perfect gimlet, an outer-borough Magellan who'd drive us miles for the best vindaloo. There was one I brought to a family wedding who could, mirabile dictu, actually swing dance.

Yet I kept them all at swing-dance-partner distance. Involved, enjoying, doing my best to coordinate, but somehow at a slightly stiffened arm's length. I didn't always know why, exactly. But when I was debating breaking up with Magellan, a friend of mine asked, by way of diagnosis, "Do you feel like you want to run things by him?" Genius! This, to me, was the million-dollar question. 'Cause the answer was no. I liked him, but I didn't look up to him; I enjoyed him, but I didn't need to know what he thought. He wasn't the older brother guy from my childhood. He wasn't going to be my shoulder, my rock, my go-to. He just wasn't. Nor were the others.

Anyway, I still had my parents for that.

By the time I decided to go through with any given breakup, I was sure of myself. But along the way, I'd worry: Am I just getting "I'm special" on these poor guys' asses? Am I waiting not for a guy who's good enough for me, but who's good enough to take an only child away from her parents? In which case I'll be waiting till the Red Sox win the World Series.

Oh, wait.

I met David at a party in Manhattan. Leave it to homebody me:

Turned out his apartment was literally around the corner from mine, so close we could have watched each other's TVs. It got serious fast. I could tell because we were always together; I could tell because messages from Mom were going unanswered. Why? Not only because David and I were in the fall-off-the-face-of-the-earth stage of love, but also because I didn't have that much to say to her. How should I deal with this crazy editor? I'd ask David. Can you proofread this angry letter to the *Times*? I'd ask David. How do you keep brisket from drying out? I'd ask David's mom.

Mom fought back, a little. When I brought him home for Passover—proud, triumphant, *this time I mean it!*—she took me aside and told me, with great and sincere concern, that I was being "too much." Too excited around him. Too loud, too funny, too me. That I, in all my it's-all-about-me, see-how-special-I-am exuberance, might "scare him away."

I didn't speak to her for a week. She can frown on my hair-color choices, but how *dare* she burst that bubble? At some level, though—even though Mom and I never acknowledged this when we made up—I knew what was going on. My earlier radio silence had tipped her off, and now that she'd seen us together, she knew: He was different. Special. Possibly even special enough. She was grasping at me as I slipped, laughing and twirling, away.

Eight months later, at our wedding, my parents made a toast. "David, you are special, and we believe you treasure the specialness in Lynn," they said together. "We hand Lynn over to you with trust, with love, with joy, and with the strong sense that the two of you will now bloom together." After our honeymoon, I called them from the cab, just to let them know we'd landed safely.

Odd Numbers

Thomas Beller

I. We're Splitting Up

THE TURBULENCE BEGAN when his girlfriend broke up with him. Two weeks later the phone rang.

"I was at home, a little tipsy. You know. Because of the girlfriend," said my friend.

It was afternoon. We were on the sidewalk. We'd almost said good-bye, but then I asked him how he was, and he started delivering these fragments.

"And I got this call," he continued. "Both parents on the line. And they never do that, both of them on the line like that. And my dad, he says these words I never ever thought I'd hear. He goes, 'We're splitting up.' Like that. Real matter of fact. I asked when it happened. I was in shock. They said that it's been coming for about fifteen years or something. It was a total shock. I had no idea. And now I want to know everything. I want all the details, all the facts. It's happening, like, right away. She's moving out at the end of the month."

"You have brothers and sisters?" I asked.

"Two younger sisters."

"You guys must be in serious conference mode."

"Totally. But it's also really complicated, because of the way it was handled. It wasn't handled very well. They wanted to tell the youngest one in person. She was coming home a couple of days after they called me. So I had to wait to talk to her, so they could tell her in person."

"But you had the middle one," I said.

"Yeah. We could talk right away. But it was awkward, because we couldn't talk to the youngest one, who was about to graduate from college, so she had that going on, and I had to sort of duck her for a few days because there was no way I was going to have a conversation with my youngest sister and pretend that this bombshell was not about to drop."

"That's crazy," I said. "You had no idea? They seemed happy?"

"It honestly never occurred to me that something was wrong between my parents. And then they say, 'It's been in the works on and off for about fifteen years.'"

"And then what happened?" I said. "I mean after you got off the phone. What did you do? Did you call anyone? The middle sister?"

"No. I didn't call her. I didn't call anyone. I just went out and got really drunk. I was tipsy when I got the call. But then I went out and got drunk."

"With a friend?" I asked.

"Oh, no. No." He chuckles. "Alone."

"Good!" I said, for some reason, as though this was the heroic way to handle it—alone in a bar, misery in the romantic style. I was struggling to see the bright side of things, as I often do, by exaggerating the dark side of things, a reflexive making light of things when confronted with pain.

He looked at me as though he was beyond this. "Good!" I might have more to say. Or maybe he was merely gathering himself after having just recollected that night.

"That's so awful," I continued, shifting gears. "I mean, it's almost like they waited for all the kids to graduate from college, and then their job was done."

But then I had to stop this line of thought. I was headed somewhere along the lines of "At least you got into your mid-twenties and have become this cool, relatively together guy. At least your parents stayed together until all the kids had graduated from college. At least it didn't happen when you were twenty! Or fifteen! Or ten! Or two!"

But this is an absurd way of thinking, I told myself, a kind of cost-benefit analysis applied to emotional pain, in which you gauge how much the bad news, whatever it is, hampers psychic and economic and romantic productivity.

So I told him how it was cool that he had gotten drunk by himself. There's a real romance to being at a bar alone with your misery and getting drunk. It works on a stoop with a bottle of beer or whatever, too. I told him to hang in there, and remarked that it really did sound like a "rough spring." It was the most private conversation we'd had. We parted ways with a "see you later," and that was that. Soon we'd go back to talking about literature, and the project we were working on, and whatever else.

As I left him that afternoon, I found myself thinking about how, even if it did totally suck to have your parents on the line both at the same time, in a way that they never did before, itself a weird kind of togetherness that would be the first of an ensuing avalanche of annoying little ironies since its purpose was to announce an apartness—even in the face of this major bummer, he still had his two sisters to talk to. I found myself fantasizing briefly about the angsty, whispery conversations that would take place among them.

Surely they were really smart and cool, like he was, and maybe less prone to these gnomic little exclamations, which is how he spoke. It would be a real bonding experience for them, is what I thought, and I found myself thinking of Jonathan Franzen's *The Corrections* and those three remote, fucked-up siblings, who nevertheless were part of a web of experience that they all shared, each with their own variation on their shared perspective (from below) on those huge, totemic figures known as parents. Each a witness to one another's lives. At one point in that novel, Chip, the youngest and most overtly desperate of the crew, finds himself bitching at one of his students, whom he has been sleeping with. She is an only child and can't shut up about what a great relationship she has with her parents, who are progressive-minded millionaires and who home-schooled her until she was twelve or something. At one point he shouts something like "You're supposed to rebel against your parents, not be buddies with them, that's how you become a person!"

When I first read that line I agreed feverishly before remembering that I myself have somehow managed to do both at the same time, befriended and rebelled, more or less. But maybe I've been fooling myself.

Now, hearing this guy's bad news, I found myself thinking it was really great that he had siblings. He could talk to them. Together, they could try and unravel the mysteries of their parents' marriage. I was thinking that even if it was terrible to get this news of his parents' sudden (from his point of view) divorce, at least he had the others. They could help one another! They could soften the blow. Then I remembered that no one can really soften the blow.

And then I realized that all these thoughts about how lucky he was that he had siblings were a complete reversal from a long-held opinion I'd had that siblings tend to fall somewhere on the spectrum between annoying and complete hell. It was a vaguely formed opinion, sort of stupid, but based on empirical evidence. The siblings of my friends had always seemed like an ordeal, a laborious chore, and, more than occasionally, a form of torture.

Until now.

II. It's Hell, but It's Worth It

We live in a database age. We can sort by topic. We can sort by neighborhood and by skin color, and by the nations you have visited recently. We can sort by least expensive and most expensive. We can sort by people who like grape soda, and those who like orange soda, and those who used to like grape soda but who for some reason almost never drink it, either because it is too sweet or because the taste of grape soda takes them back to earlier years when they drank it all the time, years that are so sticky-sweet and confused that a single sip of grape soda, besides providing a kind of bottomless blast of grape flavor, also contains a huge amount of information that you might not want thrust into the forefront of your thoughts. (I'm in this last group.)

The database subsets are endless. It's incredibly satisfying, this parsing by category, and at the same time it is incredibly obtuse.

I'm against it, even as I enjoy it. So here is a book that sorts according to "siblings: 0." I can't stand the thought of using being an only child as a prism through which to view experience. Why not? Because I don't want to be a category. I don't want a label. I'M SPECIAL!

Special, though, is a two-way street. There is "unique, talented, and charming" special, and "uncanny ability to throw round ball into hoop" special. And there is "math for idiots" special, "You will never slow dance at camp" special, "Please come to the remedial batting practice session while everyone else gets to play" special.

I belong to the group composed of people who don't want to be part of a group. Beneath my defensiveness on the matter, however, is another defensiveness, which has to do with a very simply stated part of my biography—my father died when I was around ten. I hate the one-lineness of this. I'm sure I am projecting anger about the fact onto the simplicity of this fact, its bluntness. You announce this fact, that your father died when you were young, and all of a sudden anyone can look at some attribute of yours, good or bad, and find a way to trace it back to this point of origin, and your personal tragedy now becomes a kind of voodoo doll to be poked at by anyone who wants to try their hand at on-the-spot psychoanalysis.

All of this reluctance to talk about my childhood from the point of view of the child would have kept me from writing this essay altogether, probably, were it not for a new and totally radical concept that recently occurred to me—thinking about being an only child from the point of view of a parent.

At this point in my life, the only children I know are only children. Right away, in the very act of writing about it, the unified, solitary, self-referential reality of being an only child asserts itself—you can't write a sentence about them without the sentence becoming a hall of self-referential mirrors.

I only know only children mostly because my friends with one kid haven't had the time to have two. They're just recovering from the first.

Whether they have the inclination to have another will become apparent. Sooner or later.

One couple with whom my fiancée and I are friends has a cute little tyrant, Chris. Sometimes we visit with Chris for an hour or so before his bedtime, an event the father refers to as "the Execution." This is because of the screams.

I like this couple a lot. We always go to their place, and they always put out an excellent spread of cheese, salami, and so on. Chris's parents treat us with a tender solicitude that, I notice, often comes to us, the engaged couple, from married couples a few notches further along than us. The theme of this solicitude and goodwill was always along the lines of "It's hell, but it's worth it."

It was never clear what "it" was. Life, perhaps. Marriage. Children. Bedtime. Everything.

Then one day we got a call. Our arrangements with Chris's parents were always casual, a bit last minute, but this invitation had a note of urgency.

"How about tonight?" they said.

"Sure," we said. "We're free," we said. "Why not?"

I started looking forward to the salami, the cheeses, the pâté, the ambient light of their tastefully renovated apartment, the conversation. We came over in time for the Execution, which was delayed by our arrival. Then it was time for bed. Chris's screams weren't too bad. We all collapsed in the living room. Now we were in the two-couple constellation, a mode of socializing that I had grown to feel so drawn to since getting engaged. I felt like I was getting pulled into a giant conspiracy, the conspiracy of the married, and I liked it. The distinguishing feature of this two-couple format was the interesting tension that brings everyone close, and holds them there, close but not too close, almost levitating in the mysterious air of friendship—that mode of experience, that relationship, which had once meant the world to me, but now, in comparison to the bonds of marriage, and the duties of parenthood, seemed like a light thing, like a magnifying glass you picked up and played with for a while, before putting it back down.

"So, Tom," said Chris's mom. "We were wondering."

Where would she go from here? For a moment I was giddy with the possibilities. She could be wondering about anything.

"What was it like to grow up in the city as an only child?" she asked.

"I don't know," I said. I was a bit taken aback. "Hard to know how to separate the only from the childhood."

"Because we think we might only have one," said the dad. "Because we've been trying and—"

"We might adopt," she said.

"Or we might not," he said. "We've been thinking about it and—"

"We wanted to know," she said. "What it was like."

I pictured them in a mode of extreme anxiety on the subject and then one of them saying, "Elizabeth's fiancé was an only child; let's ask him!"

Or would they have said, ". . . *is* an only child"? When do you stop being one?

"I'm not sure what to say," I said. They may as well have asked what it was like to breathe the air in New York as a kid. What was breathing it like? How might you have been different if you breathed something else? I don't know. It was air. I breathed it. I suppose I knew there was other air, elsewhere. But I didn't really think about it.

Now I stared at the anxious faces of my new friends. I wanted to help.

In their eyes, just then, I registered the fatigue of trying to have a second kid and not being able to, and also a more abstract fatigue of distinguishing between doing what was best for them and doing what was best for their son, who was part of them, but who was also, irrefutably, as with all children, someone else. It's one thing to give up trying to have a kid. Quite another if you feel you are somehow depriving the one kid you have.

Could I recommend being an only child?

"I don't know what to tell you," I said, "I kind of liked it, I think. It's the childhood I had. A brother and sister, it's impossible to imagine. But I'll tell you this, I felt very loved."

III. All the Love

I brought it up with a friend who is a parent of an only child. My friend does not live with the mother of his child anymore. (A bit clinical, that phrase, "mother of his child," but "wife" no longer applies.) So this only child is not a temporary only child, he's the only kid these two people are going to have.

"It's not a problem for him, being an only child, is it?" I asked.

"Hmmm," my friend said, making a face, as though to say, "You're a little off, but really, I'd rather not even get into it."

"Think of all the love he gets," I said. "He gets all the love!"

"Yeah, they get all the love," said my friend. "But then they have trouble when they get to school and have to compete for attention with all the other kids, and they can't handle it; they've never had to compete for attention before. So it's not so great."

I was like, "Hey! What do you mean it's not so great!?"

IV. You Could Make a Circle

When I was a little kid, I wanted a brother. I wanted him a lot. Eventually, after relentless lobbying had not produced a brother, I said I would settle for a sister. Then, a dog. But my mother was allergic to dogs and cats. And the brother and the sister did not come because my father got sick. So it was just me.

I started liking it. At times, I loved it. I loved being an only child! School was, for all kinds of reasons, total hell. Was that because I was an only child? I can't imagine it was. School was hell. At home, it was great, or, at the least, it was private, and I liked the privacy. Is a taste for solitude something one develops in reaction to the necessity of being alone a lot? Or is being alone a happy thing when you have a taste for solitude?

I know about my sibling longing in the abstract, from stories my mother has told me. It's not a memory I really possess on my own. Mostly I remember liking the silences. The stillness. I loved our apartment, loved its nooks and crannies and the quiet of it and the light. And when my dad died, it got more quiet, and the light became more mystical, and life, weirdly enough, went on. I often had the place to myself.

• • •

WHEN MY FATHER was alive, we were a family of three. Then, after my father died, it was just two of us. Three is an odd number. But two, if the two is composed of a mother and a son, is also an odd number.

I protected our place from others. I protected the apartment. I kept it to myself. I socialized elsewhere. I'm moving toward a somewhat overdetermined point—after all, I wrote a novel called *The Sleep-Over Artist*—but the flip side to my spending a lot of time at other people's houses was that I didn't want to have them at my own house.

Why? There was nothing really to be ashamed of. It had the personality of my parents, which at a certain age is appalling because it just is.

Beyond that, I don't know. My neighbor and good friend Rich came over once with a friend from school. As they were leaving, my dad said, "Wait, hold on, what's that?"

He pointed to Rich's friend, to the bulge underneath his shirt.

The kid said, "What? What?"

"That," said my father. He pointed.

"What?"

We were in the narrow hallway. A weird little dance ensued in the narrow space, as the kid did a slow turn away from the pointing finger, as if he were trying to turn around and see the back of his head. "What? What? What?"

Eventually, the bulge was shown to be my baseball glove. The kid was trying to steal it. Right out of my house! A kind of sickening confusion settled over me, and Rich and his friend left. My dad handed me the mitt.

A few years later Rich came over again with another friend. In those years I was at Rich's house all the time. I was practically a member of his family. They were so generous. The sheer cost of feeding me must have been enormous. Now here was a rare visit to my place, and why not? It was maybe fifteen steps from his front door.

Like the last time, Rich's friend was not someone I knew.

They did something that made me want them to leave. I don't remember what it was. I suspect it was nothing, just a feeling, a voice raised too loud, something that made me want them to go. I'm not entirely sure my dad was dead at that point, though I think he was. My mom wasn't home.

It was just us. So much time in the apartments of my youth was independent time, ear cocked for the sound of the lock. The key to the pleasure was that I was alone in there. I loved that feeling, except now I was not alone, and I had been provoked. Some small bit of anarchy had been set loose in our apartment. I wanted them to leave. But they didn't.

"Get out!" I said. But they wouldn't.

The apartment had an odd layout. There was a long hallway that ran parallel to a room—we called it "the study," but I suppose it could have been a dining room or a bedroom—that had two doors on either end. What this meant was you could make a circle.

What happened when Rich and his friend, the stranger, wouldn't leave is that I started to chase them. Of course, as soon as I did this it became a game, and they started running away from me and laughing. I chased them down the hall—they ran ahead, turned right, back through the study, then right again, down the hall, a loop. Thundering kid feet, six legs running, like drums, six big marching-band bass drums, *thud thud thud thud*. A stampede.

At some point, after a couple of laps, I got a knife. I went to the kitchen, got a big steak knife, and started running after them screaming, "Get out of my house! Get out of my house!"

I remember their thudding feet and laughter, and I remember the choking rage I felt as I chased them. It was the rage from a dream—disturbed, outsize, murderous in that emotionally naked way one can experience feelings in a dream. Except this knife was real.

Eventually, they left. The place became quiet again.

THIS MEMORY CAME back to me with an odd forcefulness recently, when my mother threw an engagement party for me and my fiancée. The party was great. It was a mixture of my fiancée's friends and my own. Some of her friends hardly knew me, really, and they had certainly never met my mother, let alone been in her home. But even among my friends, especially the ones I have made since college, many of them have never really met my mother.

And the apartment? Forget it. A couple of college buddies had seen it twenty years earlier, and that was it. It's not like I was keeping my mother a secret. But hardly anyone had been to the apartment.

The day of the engagement party, I got there early and helped set up. My mother, in an unusual moment of delegation, had ordered some platters of cheese and things like that, and they had been delivered. She covered the tables with white cloths, and she set out lots of flowers. I put out the platters: large plastic carousels of food made by others. They seemed foreign in that handmade house, but welcome; it meant my mother could just be there at the party, too.

It was a bright summer afternoon, a lot of light. My fiancée,

Elizabeth, was getting ready downtown. She would come later. There was a weird moment when I realized I was all grimy from running around, and so I showered there for the first time in more than a decade. Showering at the ancestral home on the day of your engagement party. My old bathroom was filled with stuff— a lot of dry cleaning was hanging above the bathtub, and it wasn't dry cleaning in play, by which I mean that the clothes weren't things my mother still wore. They were things that she didn't wear anymore, but had gotten cleaned, as though in a clean condition their fate would be easier to determine. I had long since given up on discussing the rationale for such gestures. But what this meant was that it was my mom's shower that I used, my mom's shampoo, her conditioner. The water poured over me. My dad had stood here once, I thought. I shaved, and I remembered watching him shaving in this same mirror. He had used a different kind of razor, the kind where you replaced the whole blade. I was using a very modern device. He would have been impressed. The razors had changed. How about the faces?

The guests began to arrive. One after another. Bright eyes and open smiles. Some brought things—I had made several last-minute panicked calls for more white wine. Everyone seemed happy.

And yet I realized there was an odd knot in my chest that transcended the usual host anxiety, and probably went a bit beyond the nature of the occasion. All these strangers were in my mother's house! They were just . . . here!

And it was fine!

No one fainted at the sight of its particulars. To the extent they noticed the house at all, they thought it was nice, and beyond that, people were wrapped up in the happy occasion. Elizabeth arrived, totally glowing and, somehow, new. She seemed to have fought off wedding-planning anxiety for the time being and was just here with me.

At some point everyone crowded into the study, and there was a terrifying speech, one of those toasts that verges into a roast before retreating at the Maginot Line of tact. We stood there, Elizabeth and I, excited and freaked out. I saw the crowd of happy faces. Some were total strangers. But even among my closest friends there was a distinctly disjointed quality to seeing them in this room, which many years earlier I had raced through shouting, "Get out of my house!"

Now I was happy to have them all there, as witnesses to this evolution. My mom stood in the doorway to the crowded room, watching. The numbers were changing to another, lovely, kind of odd.

Separation and the Single Girl

Sara Reistad-Long

WHEN I WAS little, I was so enmeshed with my parents that I could imagine myself crawling inside them—fusing with them. My boundaries were blurred to the point that I would "punish" them when we argued by banging my own head against the wall. Misguided, perhaps, but effective.

As I grew up, my parents spared nothing for me, their only and last-chance child. I was showered with love, attention, toys, lessons, affirmation, and a hearty dose of pop psychology. For my mother, a brief attempt at juggling infant and career ended abruptly thanks to a tripped-out babysitter. She gave up her own promising academic and journalistic aspirations to throw herself into my development. All her intellect went into making sure I'd turn out as normal and well-adjusted as was possible for an intense, introspective little girl. Playdates were serious business, on par with Suzuki and horse camp. Ski trips were an opportunity to bring a friend and simulate a more typical family for a bit. Crowded, tomboy summers in my mother's native Sweden with my two rowdy, older, boy cousins, a chance for me to toughen up and become more self-reliant.

Still, all these orchestrated interactions were really just performances, part of a necessary script. I got to the real meaning of things early on, during one of our Sweden summers. I was five or six and had just learned to dive. My mother was so proud that she promised to take me to the nearest toy store—an hour away—that carried a particular plastic horse I'd been obsessing over. We rose at the crack of dawn for this mission because nobody could know. All the way there, she explained how important it was that I not tell a soul because this gesture showed that she loved me more than she did my cousins. Of course, I already knew that. But those words, the glow of our trip, were my real prize. And I never told. I dared not disturb the pristine memory. I went home and played loudly with my cousins. The gift remained a secret between my mother and me.

TODAY, I PLAY myself bolder and braver than maybe I am. A friend once called me the "ultimate activity partner" because, in her words, I'll try anything once, usually twice, and always in heels. But I'm afraid of stupid things, like stairs without railings. I have an easy time making, and keeping, friends. But I sometimes, suddenly, become shy and unsteady, even around those closest to me. Like nearly every other only child I've met, I prefer to be alone. However, I fear loneliness with a wild, pawing agitation.

In childhood, my greatest nightmare was my parents dying or being taken away—me waking up and having them not there. Then, in my mid-twenties, I watched my robust father survive cancer.

Frail and bald, he was wheeled into surgery after surgery. Now, that dream crawls up on me, hooks its claws, and sometimes won't let go. Having Mom and Dad waiting in the wings has made me appear enviably confident, but I suspect that when my supporting cast takes its final bow, I'll stumble more than most.

As my parents aged, and my own fears of loneliness deepened, a new perspective crept into my more serious romances: Love was great, but loyalty was paramount. I craved assurance, safety, and promises of permanence. So I tested my boyfriends and tried their patience. I wanted to know how long my leash was; if I let them in, was I at risk for later abandonment? I was raised to be my own person, freethinking and independent (ironic, considering the dependability of my safety net). But when thinking about marriage— that age-old means of recasting your primary players—I inclined toward parental, authoritative characters, men who re-created the dynamic I was most used to. Letting my boyfriends take the lead mimicked the safe, accounted-for feelings I equated with family. Even now, I catch myself yearning for whomever I happen to be dating to "take care of things." I was an older-man time bomb, and so at twenty-six, I started up with a thirty-eight-year-old Frenchman with a questionable history and two stormy marriages under his belt. The whole arrangement felt remarkably natural. I was looking for a replacement.

I MET J. at a gala event. He was the hotshot wine director of a top New York City restaurant and looked amazing—truly amazing— in a polished, shaken-not-stirred suit (with tie long discarded and two buttons open). I was wearing a knockout red dress and long silver earrings. There was magnetism. It really was one of those "from across the room" moments. In its own way, of course. At the time, I thought I was shooting him a sultry come-hither look. In hindsight, I believe it fell into the "drunk-and-available" category. We were making out within the hour. Well into our relationship, in certain circles, our how-we-met story would get that "Oh, so *you're* the girl who . . ." Classy, *bien sûr*.

Our courtship was indulgent, and our romance even more so. I'm sure he enjoyed the arm-candy factor of a younger woman, and he took pride in my Ivy League and prep-school social spheres. Only my parents would have beamed more over my achievements or professed the same eagerness to see me further my career. He called me incessantly, treated me like a princess, and told me he loved me, passionately, within weeks. I found him electrifying, thrilling, charismatic, and beautifully dangerous, but, more important, I felt safe and cared for. I couldn't get enough of his gritty stories of punk and Palladium New York in the eighties, his intelligent and remarkably observant missives from the restaurant world, and his over-the-top lifestyle. I loved the special treatment we received at expensive restaurants thanks to his job, loved bringing my friends around when he was working so we could be plied with wine and canapés like movie stars. I felt sophisticated and important going out with his older crowd, as though I'd been admitted to a special club. And, probably thanks to his years of promiscuity, the sex blew my mind.

There was a darker side. He had a temper. Drugs were de rigueur, far removed from the banker blow I was used to. And, in trying to keep up with the big boys, I was already starting to drink heavily. But J.'s doting attention overshadowed everything else. I was in a tremendously unstructured period in my life, having recently left a stable job to be an unstable full-time writer. Our domestic routine was comforting. He offered to provide a cushion if my finances were ever tight. When I first went freelance, my father had made that promise, too, but I felt so much safer knowing I had an "emergency contact" here in the city, as opposed to miles away in North Carolina. And J. covered our joint expenses, which added up. He explained to me that these were things *he* wanted for us, like expensive trips and fancy dinners; I couldn't afford them and he could, so it was no problem, he said, for him to pay. Eventually, that scope expanded to clothes and trinkets for me. I was skeptical at first, but I accepted them with less and less thought about what doing so might mean.

J. adored me with a near-obsessive single-mindedness. He petted me, coddled me, worried when I wore impractical shoes in the rain, and became my hero forever by slowly, slowly guiding me down not one but three Mayan temples that I'd climbed in a series of misguided acts of courage during a Central American vacation. I reciprocated by throwing myself into the housewife role laid out for me: editing his lectures, fussing over the apartment, shuffling my schedule and projects to fit the social obligations he made for us, and delighting in giving him the unconditional love he said he'd never had. I felt as though I were sharing the overflow of attention I'd always received.

"Show me the ring and I'll meet the man" was my father's party line on boyfriends. In my experience, this worked well for everyone involved. So I was caught completely off guard when, six months into our relationship, J. became furious when he learned that my dad was coming for a weekend and I hadn't thought to arrange an introduction. I suppose it *is* a little unusual, the way my father deals with my love life. I used to try to force things, turn him into the guy who holds the key to my tower, but it's just not how he perceives his role. He identifies with me so intensely that the idea of controlling me is probably abhorrent to him. As for meeting outsiders, he'd rather hear me weave the stories. We have a little world, the three of us, and we all nurse it in our own ways.

In this case, though, I felt backed against a wall. And so, after a bit of coaxing and a few tears, my father agreed to brunch. But J., nervous, insisted on dinner. At his restaurant. When he was working. He must have thought that he could better impress in his own element. After all, countless moguls, stars, and other heavyweights revered his opinions on wine. Surely, he must have thought, this was a home-run strategy. But having your father waited on—both literally and figuratively—by your boyfriend is bizarre, unnerving, and ugly. Particularly when your boyfriend seems a tongue slip away from calling your dad "sir." J. had never fumbled around me. He was always self-assured and had an uncanny way of knowing how to take care of things. Now he was awkward and stammering, and compensating for it all by showering us with more and more expensive, meaningless food and wine. I felt unhinged. I hadn't counted on this. I drank everything in front of me to get away. I don't remember much, but I do remember my dad taking me home and telling me, "Daughter, you may think you can, but you sure don't know how to handle your liquor." I hate that memory.

Even after that bumpy incident, my father did his best to stay neutral. But my mother, already on edge, was becoming frantic. J. was talking marriage, and, despite my assurances that I "wasn't there yet," she was itching to get me as far away from him as she could. On my end, I was confused. For all her intensity, she had always made a point of leaving my personal life alone. This must have felt more real to her. Maybe when you have more kids, you can be a little more patient about these things. Parents don't want to be alone, either; when you've got one shot, any sign of dissent has got to be unnerving.

Still, she could have better controlled her panic. Her frequent visits were fraught with tension, and even though I lived with the man for the better part of a year, she refused to meet him. J. responded in kind. Theirs was a relationship of bitter, growling mistrust. Indeed, both my parents' attention was becoming worried, alarmed, our conversations terse and strained. For the first time in my life I felt alienated from them; neither camp could accept the other's position. J. was charismatic, I was in love, and our little Upper East Side nest made up for the support I felt I was losing. I liked the safety of an established, well-run ship. Even more so when I had it all to myself, when J. was away and I was in control within its boundaries. I was starting to consider this marriage a possibility, if not a likelihood. Still, I never stopped calling my mother every day, more so when J. would yell at me, which he did increasingly often. On good days, I was distant, guarded. On bad ones I floundered, searching for an anchor. To be the person on the receiving end of either variant must have been torture.

J.'s background was very different from mine. He'd had a fairly rough and often lonely—not to mention shady—past. As a result, he was as independent and suspicious of others as I was needy and trusting. It was a bad combination. Under a great deal of work stress, he became more and more irritable and angry. He had a different story for everyone. I'd catch him in untruths but hold my tongue. I had little experience with heated confrontation, so our arguments evolved into a pattern of yelling on his end and sobbing on mine. Always at night, always boozy, sometimes in public, and always followed by intense, even violent sex. In the morning, I'd wake up next to the most charming, tender man in the world. One night, a passing stranger caught me from behind, stuck his hand up my dress, and grabbed me—hard—as I was standing outside my door fumbling for the keys. When I got home J. lit into me for nearly an hour, telling me I deserved it for the way I dressed. The next day he took me to Balthazar and later helped me file the police report. My friends started calling him Dr. Jekyll and Mr. Hyde. I knew that our relationship was unhealthy, but I always managed to make up excuses, adjusting my own mind to understand his. I convinced myself that he needed me. The truth was that I'd become too dependent on him to cut things off. In my mind, he was taking care of me, and both he and I believed that I'd be helpless without him.

I wish I could say I was the one who got up the nerve to leave him. I'd tried a few times, but never made it past a day or two. So, finally, he left me.

This was new territory. Nobody had ever walked out on me before. I was crushed. From then on, he popped in and out of my life for a good six months. Like an alley cat, he kept coming around. And I waited patiently with the milk. Our breakup devolved into a more extreme version of how we'd been when we were together. The harder he dropped me, the more I needed another fix. Fittingly, I'd pass the time by keeping myself as boozed up as I possibly could. I was remarkably successful at it.

My move back into my own life was terrifying and confusing. With my friends, I'd gone from being the number one go-to girl to being the problem case. Still, when I was with them, I was able to look ahead. I truly, honestly, *did* want nothing more than to be over him and move on and be the happy, self-assured girl I'd been before. After all, I'd never intended for him to replace my friends.

But with my parents, even though I'd all but stopped working and was relying heavily on their financial support, I was angry. They were the people I'd mentally pitted against my ex. They reminded me of what I'd lost and of all the future aloneness that such a thing could mean. So I was furious with them. Of course, I still called them late at night, often after dates that didn't measure up, drunk and weeping over my loneliness.

And they weren't the only ones I was calling. My habitual enmeshment with J. had become so complete that even months after we had broken up, I actually called *him* sobbing over another boyfriend. We weren't friends at the time. Our last interactions had left me scarred and afraid of him. But in the moment I'd really forgotten all that, and dialed him without thinking, the way I do my mom.

I ALWAYS HAD *just* enough work and social engagements going to keep up appearances. But, while my feelings about myself remained ambivalent, the unbearable damage that I was doing to those around me, primarily my parents—whom I continued to lovingly resent—was what made me decide to get myself to a shrink. In typical Long family fashion, the first thing my folks wanted was his number so they could help with the process and fill in the gaps. We'd had an incident like this at the gynecologist's once, when my mom had insisted on following me in for moral support and my dad, a physician himself, had called her on her cell as my doctor was examining me to see when we'd be ready for lunch. I'm probably one of the few people in history whose father has such a vague sense of his kid's privacy that he—truly without getting the weirdness of this—has wandered down to the blood department of the clinic where he works to look over the results of my HIV test. With the therapy decision, I held firm. No numbers would be exchanged. However, when I decided I needed to learn how to control my drinking, I exhibited no more separateness from my parents than they had from me.

I wanted to sit in on a few Alcoholics Anonymous meetings. And I wanted my parents to come with me. My ordeal had, after all, been so much theirs, too. They were nervous, but didn't protest. Getting down to business, I thought it best to split the sessions. We're wacky enough individually, and as a group, like I've said, there's just a lot of us to take in. So I brought my father to my very first AA meeting. We'd hoped to just sit and listen, take it all in. But luck would not have that. *Both* of us were chosen to stand up and read aloud. Indeed, my father's assignment was to go over the twelve steps—and they don't mince words on that one. I still can't *not* get tears in my eyes when I think of my wonderful daddy—an atheist, no less—standing up in front of all those strangers and soldiering through that very, very long, dogmatically religious document for my sake. There's this part of AA where you have to introduce yourself. It's scary as hell. But I felt pretty lucky when I introduced my dad, "who's *not* an alcoholic, but he's here because we're a family, and it's really important to me that he be able to understand and be part of what I'm doing here today."

Thus began the tedious journey to find my own, independent center. My delirious relationship with J. had uncovered a deep emotional interdependence within our family that none of us really knew how to manage properly. The fact that we'd never seriously disagreed—I hadn't been a particularly rebellious kid, and they were extremely liberal parents—had until that point masked our inability to extract our discrete selves from the whole of our unit. Putting myself back together, then, meant putting up some walls. The complete vulnerability that I'd brought to the J. situation was too damaging. Just as it was dangerous to make myself so totally open to him, it was risky to lean on my parents as heavily as I had. Fear of loneliness had resulted in the worst kind of solitude—the loss of self. I needed to figure out how to keep certain things within me, to carve boundaries and places that were only mine. My parents had to learn where not to tread, and that there would likely be other times when they'd vehemently disagree with my decisions. We're still working on these things, and probably will be forever. But so far, the results are good. I think all three of us feel more balanced as individuals, and that can't help but flow over into our relationships with one another. None of this is to say that our obsession with one another has lessened even a little, as evidenced by the recent purchase of "Long-family webcams," but I'd like to think we're smarter about it now. Together, we're slowly sorting ourselves out.

BLOOD OF MY BLOOD

REBECCA WALKER

S EVERAL YEARS AGO I was walking on a tree-lined street in Larchmont, the New York suburb where I lived for a couple of years in the early eighties. As I passed the ice-cream parlor my father often took me to after dinner during the long, hot New York summers, a jogger—white, over six feet tall, with a gold chain around his neck—stopped me to talk. "David" told me that we had gone to junior high school together, and after twenty years what he remembered about me was that I had protected him from bullies.

Surprised to be face-to-face with my past, I stood squinting at the sun setting behind David's blue velour tracksuit, and scrambling to imagine a fourteen-year-old version of the twentysomething man in front of me.

"You were so tough," he continued. "Everyone was afraid of you."

"Everyone?" I shot back with the vaguest hint of sarcasm.

But David kept talking. "You lived in the Bronx before you

moved here, right?" He said that all the kids thought I would kick the butt of anyone who messed with me. He was one of my friends, and so he was left alone.

Of course, my memory being what it is, a vast and notoriously selective place, I had no recollection of protecting David from anyone. And yet I believed him because I recognized myself in his story. As we parted, giving each other a hug and a kiss on both cheeks, I wondered at my history of championing others, tucking them under my wing in times of need. I remembered putting my thesis on hold to fly across country to rescue a friend in the throes of a nervous breakdown, putting my life in danger to counsel a friend against consummating a relationship with a guy in the mob, and coming far too close to adopting the child of yet another friend who had fallen into crisis. The list of Herculean efforts, many of which were too complicated and sensitive to reveal here, was staggering.

What David told me also rang true because while I didn't remember him, I did remember my father marveling at how, in as early as eighth grade, my friends all came to me with their problems, trusting me to make sense of their adolescent angst. Because my father made a career of taking on the problems of others—clients, citizens in need, his friends and family—I felt more deeply connected to him through this common urge, and smiled proudly when he made the observation. We may not both have had curly hair, but we did both sit distracted at the family dinner table, preoccupied by the needs of others.

But when I look back on the days of rescue missions and self-defeating attempts to right the lives of others, I see something else, too. Playing the tough guy to the damsel in distress wasn't entirely about emulating my father, wasn't just about following the genetic code. It was also about how vulnerable and alone I felt after my parents' divorce, and how much I needed someone to shield me from my fears and translate what was happening into terms I could understand. The truth is that by rearranging my mouth and shoulders, by writing a good script that I followed to the letter, I became the strapping, protective big brother I longed for. Tough, in charge, intuitive, and altruistic, I manifested exactly the kind of person that I hoped would appear.

The people I saved, or tried to save, or thought I was saving, were all me. They were the me I didn't know how to articulate, the me that needed an intimate other—blood of my blood, flesh of my flesh—to swoop down into my only-child life and make sense of things. How we were going to live in two places instead of one, for example. Or how our parents could still love us if they didn't love each other. I probably romanticized the idea of a sibling, but I thought that if I could just share my grief over the tear in the fabric that was my life, I had a real shot at surviving it.

I CLUNG TO my girlfriends. I was always crossing some unspoken line with them, too, entering into relationships that were too close, too *intimate*. Unlike David, whom I did not remember, I do remember the names and faces of those girls, the way our enmeshments were tinged with drama and heat. Donna, Heide, Tina, Jamie, Malaika, Lauren. I had met each one, fallen in love with her, and then grabbed her up and held on tight. Too tight. I didn't have any way to measure the distance between us, no real sister at home to provide an accurate gauge of the precise increments between friend and family. As a result, there was an odd friction in the relationships, an unspoken tension about how close we should be. I wanted something permanent, forever. They had that with their siblings at home.

Last year I was at a university in New Orleans, teaching with a program that gives cameras to kids to document and better understand their lives. Remembering that one of the girlfriends I thought I would know forever—I'll call her June—lived in the area and had just had a baby, I sent her an e-mail inviting her to lunch. Within hours, we were at Whole Foods, cautiously checking out who the other had become.

June was older and thinner, and completely and understandably absorbed in her child. She had changed her first name, and spoke with what was either a newly acquired Southern drawl or a medication-induced slur. She mentioned her husband's name emphatically every few sentences, and also the names of her horses. She had a brittle, distracted way about her, and after just a few minutes of eating free-range drumsticks under an outdoor umbrella, I found myself growing increasingly worried about her mental health.

In a previous life I would have reached in, asked the pertinent questions, and offered myself as a soft landing for whatever wasn't going right. On that day, I exercised the newfound restraint of the recovered, monitoring my feelings rather than acting on them. It was hell because what I felt was shock and grief. I was shocked by the sobering reality of our relationship, and filled with grief about the death of my illusions about it.

Because obviously, and this really did bowl me over at the time, the woman sitting in front of me was in no way related to me. There was no need for us to continue to be connected, no reason to shoot yearly e-mails back and forth. She had gone right where I went left, south where I went north. The connection I thought we had, the connection I, in fact, still felt sitting at Whole Foods more than fifteen years later, no longer existed. And as I listened to this stranger talk about what she had made of her life, and as I heard myself offer some distorted, off-key version of my own, I began to wonder if our connection had *ever* existed in the way I imagined it. Had I made it all up? The pact to talk through any problem, come at every call, and to, no matter how much time had lapsed, start wherever we had left off?

Later that night in my tiny apartment for teachers in residence, I lay awake thinking about the encounter. June's husband, who had picked us up and dropped me off on their way home, didn't remember my name or look me in the eye. Her little girl, a blond, doe-eyed child, had eyed me with what could only be described as hostility from her booster seat in the back. Was it racial? It was, after all, the South and June was white and I was not. Was June's marriage falling apart? I would never know. What I did know was that our relationship, June's and mine, was pretty much over. Without the sister fantasy, the self-created myth that water was at least as thick as blood, there was nothing to keep us together.

I HAD BEEN trying unsuccessfully to make friends into family for twenty-five years when I fell in love with S., my partner, my guy, the father of my son. In the early days of our relationship, S. was more than a little alarmed at the degree of influence my friends had on my life. When I explained that my friends were not just friends, they were family, he frowned, raised his eyebrows, and asked what was wrong with my real family. I thought he was hopelessly retrograde and unhip for asking such a question, and maybe a little bit jealous. Didn't he know that I was an only child and this was how only children made siblings? Didn't he know that friends were the new family like forty was the new thirty? What was he trying to do, anyway? Control me by separating me from the people I loved?

I initially blew off S.'s concerns, but over weeks and months they continued to arise, especially when I spent hours talking one of my friends through a crisis instead of writing or working out. Or when something a friend said pitted me against S. in an argument, effectively coming between us. Or when I couldn't make an important decision about our life together without spending hours on the phone, poring over every aspect and implication with a friend three thousand miles away.

With gentle persistence, S. continued to probe the seemingly impenetrable allegiance I had to my friends. What had they done, he wanted to know, what merit had they accumulated, to afford them the designation of family? Had they supported me through crises at great risk to themselves, made enormous sacrifices of their time and energy on my behalf, or used their resources to bring me closer to realizing my goals? Were they helping to facilitate my dream of giving birth and having a stable family of my own, or reciprocating the constant support I gave them and that I needed in order to be successful on my own terms?

The more I looked at it, the more I had to acknowledge that S. had a point. He was doing all the things he asked about, and yet I held him outside of my "family," privileging people I loved, but who, in the final analysis, always went home to their real families, the mothers and fathers, sisters and brothers, and husbands,

wives, and lovers to whom they were forever and inextricably connected. It dawned on me that while I often referred to my dear,
beloved friends as my family, they often referred to me as their
dear, beloved friend. I also considered the fact that as long as I had
a family of friends, I had a fantastic excuse not to make a family of
family.

I MADE SOME adjustments, and a year later had the miraculous
good fortune to give birth to our son, a beefy powerhouse of a boy
with a smile so outrageously big, it lights up my whole life. Now
that I have this precious, vulnerable being—blood of my blood,
flesh of my flesh—to care for, my criteria for family have shifted. I
am learning, step-by-step, the sacred dance of protection, of healthy
boundaries, of, as one friend offered while advising me to guard
that which I found most precious, "building a fence around the
Torah." I still believe in the great human family, the idea that we
are all related, that friends are family and family are friends, but
this belief is no longer borne of a desperate attempt to fill the hole
where my real family should be. Instead, it comes from a deep respect for the many different layers of relatedness, the infinite
number of gradations between human beings.

The lonely and frightened only child has given way to someone
bigger, something vast. I no longer hold on tight, but find freedom
in letting go.

DODGING LAURIE

DAPHNE UVILLER

L ET'S SAY MY parents had gone ahead and adopted the little girl they had lined up, the midwestern embryo they were about to sign for when they discovered my mom was finally, finally, joyously pregnant with yours truly. For a few seconds they toyed with the idea of keeping both her and me, as insurance, but in the end, my uncle the obstetrician convinced them that they should trust in my sticking powers.

Now let's imagine life with . . . let's call her Laurie, the name that as a child I thought was the most beautiful in the world (Susan Dey's character in *The Partridge Family* was the root of my affection). Let's imagine the following scenario if Laurie had been around.

One Friday night, when I was seventeen, maybe eighteen, my parents took off to spend the weekend at our country house, an hour and a half north of New York City, while my boyfriend and I stayed in town.

Okay, right away that gives the wrong impression. First of all, the "country house" was a soulful but ramshackle wooden two-story dwelling on stilts that my dad built when I was two and which we shared with the squirrels in the wall and the mice who left droppings in the flatware drawer, a place where you could see glimmers of sunlight through the floorboards, reflecting off the mountainside beneath the house, a place that I loved with all my heart. Second, "stayed in town" sounds pretty casual, like my parents regularly toodled off, oblivious to their teenage daughter's whereabouts. But much attention was paid to our divergent plans. In fact, it's likely that my dad, whose life was a well-examined event, held forth with a moving speech about how I no longer automatically spent the weekends with them. He may have even raised a glass to the milestone. Furthermore, although this was before the age of cell phones, I'm certain we all assumed that half a dozen communiqués were to take place by landline throughout the course of the weekend.

I can't remember if the boyfriend, whose six and a half years' seniority prompted my friends to christen him Gramps (he was all of twenty-three), had his own apartment yet or what, but there we were, spending the night at my house. And because I still had bunk beds in my room, we shacked up in my parents' room. We did this on the few occasions they weren't around, and I always assumed they assumed that's what we did. But I never exactly came right out and asked them if it was okay. In fact, I never got around to mentioning it at all. I didn't want them thinking about my "sleeping" habits more than they already did. To wit, "I'd rather you have sex for the first time under my roof, and not in some dreary dorm room, so you feel that we're here for you," said my mother when the blessed act was finally on the horizon. My parents and I embody the liberal elite; we are the folks who scare other folks into voting for Bush men.

On this particular Friday night, it rained. Hard. And it was very foggy. On this particular night, Gramps not only locked the apartment door, but also locked the door to my parents' bedroom, where we were sleeping, because he had grown up in an apartment building with a doorman and thought it was creepy that in my brownstone there was no one and nothing between us and any crazy on the street except two, now three, locked doors. We went to bed.

The next morning, Gramps went down the hall to use the bathroom. He was wearing—how do you say . . . ?—nothing. When he tried the bathroom door, he found it locked and a voice very much resembling my mother's called out, "Just a minute!" He hurried back to the bedroom, no doubt locking the door again with especial vigor, and reported this development to me. If to this point I have sounded casual about our sleeping arrangement, let's up this jig now. A crash of nervous adrenaline hit my stomach and heart and I threw on my clothes at firefighter speed, preparing half a dozen excuses—though what could they have been? We forgot how to get to my bedroom? The bunk beds were broken? We're just having breakfast in there? I raced down the hall so that my parents wouldn't actually witness me emerging from their bedroom, and nearly crashed into my mother, coming out of the bathroom. Before I could say a word, she broke into a big smile and said, "Daph, don't worry, this is *funny!*" Turns out it had been dangerously foggy on the highway, so they turned around. And when they couldn't get into their own bedroom, they slept in my bunk beds. My six-and-a-half-foot-tall father, the distinguished law professor, slept in my bunk bed while my boyfriend and I whooped it up in his bed. Hilarious.

Now, if Laurie had been in the picture, I never would have been in my parents' bedroom in the first place, because she would have told on me. Either because she never had boyfriends and was jealous of me, or because she was always the one with the boyfriends, whereas I was the nerdy one and this was an intolerable breach of the established order. Or we would have had a big fight about who got to sleep in there while they were gone, with or without boyfriends. Or we never would have been home alone in the first place because who's going to trust two teenage girls alone in the city on a Friday night? Especially when they fight all the time. No, Laurie and I both would have been in the backseat of the car when my parents—I mean *our* parents—decided to turn around. And maybe we would have had a bonding moment of eye rolling over their timidity about driving in the rain. But then we would have fought over who was willing to take the wheel. Though, growing up in New York City, neither of us would have had our driver's licenses yet, so maybe we wouldn't have had that particular fight.

In other words, the great Bedroom Swap of '89 never would have happened. Which, as I continue to cringe seventeen years later, wouldn't have been such a grievous loss to my memory bank. But my parents' lighthearted reaction to the Swap is a terrific example of two ways that my life was vastly improved by Laurie's nonarrival. No, make that three ways.

First, would my mother have been so calm and amused by the situation if she had had two comings-of-age to occupy her? Would my dad have welcomed Gramps to the breakfast table that morning with a hot cup of coffee and the *New York Times*, just happy to have a few windfall hours with his beloved daughter and her charming beau? Wouldn't my parents' parenting have, by necessity, developed into a one-size-fits-all philosophy that they applied, in the name of democracy, in broad strokes? Wouldn't they have had to say that no one gets to have sex with anyone before college, or no one gets to stay in the city alone on the weekend, regardless of who might have been mature enough to handle either of those situations?

Instead, their amused response was a way for them to project their extreme confidence in me and in my judgment. It was a rare day that went by in which my parents didn't tell me I was smart, beautiful, wise, kind, talented, or generous. All of which was very energizing to hear on a regular basis, better than any protein shake, and I highly recommend it as a parenting technique. But there was no way they could offer hard evidence to back up those statements. Proving their confidence in me, though—that they could and did do in spades. By turning over the hunk of change they had saved for me when I was eighteen and saying, Here, pay your tuition or buy a Ferrari, we trust you to make the right decision. By instructing me not to have my grades sent home from college: "We'll hear if you flunk out, and in the meantime your job is not to impress your professors, but to let them impress knowledge upon you."

Might not a sibling have undermined or at least diluted that sure-footedness? Wouldn't I have wasted precious energy trying to emerge from Laurie's shadow because she was a better student/ athlete/musician? Wouldn't I have lost hundreds of perfectly contented hours spent reading, watching television, and inventing, with my best friend, Lizzy, a game called The Price Is Always

Wrong, which involved a wet washcloth and an open window, to wondering whether there was any truth to Laurie's taunts that I was a clumsy basketball player, devoid of any fashion sense, and hopelessly unclear as to what MTV actually was? I was all those things, but so what? I didn't spend a lot of energy and therapy learning to ignore her. What a phenomenal drain on my psyche it would have been to have had someone at home who didn't adore me plain and simple. The world outside our four walls was hard enough; who needed battles at home, too? Home should be limited to teammates—only people on your side. Only people who love you unconditionally. Which, from what I can gather, siblings don't. Perhaps it's why I've always thought that a family with three or four kids was as strange an idea as a family with three or four parents (and about as fun). Each role ought to be filled once. Anything else seems like a dangerous experiment with security.

SECOND, IF LAURIE had been around to thwart the Swap, I would not have enjoyed one of the greatest boons of only-dom, which is an absence of roles. Or a condensing of them. On that absurd Saturday morning, my parents showed their willingness to accept who I was and what I was doing at any given moment without pigeonholing me by previous behavior: I was both the responsible daughter they could leave home for the weekend and the mischievous daughter, all rolled into one, with no disappointments or surprises to anyone.

I was never the pretty one or the smart one or the capable one or the lazy one or the ambitious one or the chatty one or the quiet one. I got to be all those things anytime I wanted. Because Laurie wasn't in the picture, the possibilities of what I could be were endless and endlessly changing. I could be the crunchy, peace-loving, Teva-wearing sister one day and the sardonic wiseass sister the next. Silly one day and serene the next. The discriminating gourmand one day and the lowbrow with a yen for Fluffernutters the next. Or even for dessert at the same meal. I've never had to be the one who _____, but not the one who _____. I am all of it or some of it, whenever I want to be. No temptation for my parents to label me, no sister who was already filling a role or would be envious if I did. Being an only enhanced the meaning of the word "acceptance," allowing me the freedom to be whoever I wanted to be.

On the other hand, maybe Laurie became a lawyer and maybe she earns a six-figure salary, distracting my mother from her immigrant-inherited anxieties about my writing career—am I unemployed or self-employed? Or maybe Laurie inherited my dad's gift for teaching and followed his happy footsteps into the awesome halls of academia. They have coffee and share a blueberry scone every afternoon in the faculty lounge, the highlight of his day. Certainly, Laurie didn't invent excuses to avoid playing cello-flute duets with him on Sunday mornings like I did. Even though my parents say I am everything they ever wanted, perhaps there are other things that they, as the parents of only one, cannot let themselves dare admit they might have desired.

FINALLY, MOST IMPORTANT to a one-off offspring, the Swap was indicative of my parents' willingness to share me with others. Okay, obviously, sharing me wouldn't have been an issue in the first place if they'd had the five daughters my mom says she wishes she could've had. (Crazy talk!) In that case, they would have been lucky to remember how old I was and whether I was up-to-date with my vaccinations. They would have been grateful for the two weeks every summer I spent with Lizzy's family at the beach and forever indebted to the summer camp I longed for throughout the school year. My steady stream of playdates and sleepovers—my social calendar had me keeping my own date book by age seven—would have meant one less mouth to feed. But the fact that Laurie et al were not there to fill in whenever I was absent makes it even more impressive to me that my parents, with genuine delight and enthusiasm, encouraged me to do all those things. Friends, and then boyfriends (including the ones in their bed), and, finally, that potential threat to all single-child families, a husband—all were welcomed with open arms. And, best of all, I was waved out the door without feeling I was abandoning them. Perhaps a prereq for having a happy only child is to start with a strong marriage of your own; while I was pleasantly under the impression that my parents' world revolved around me, in fact, they orbited each other with equal gravitational pull.

Because my parents have so generously shared me, I have been able to replace Laurie a thousand times over with my friends, a disproportionate number of whom (according to what study, I don't know) are also onlies. And those who aren't onlies often have brothers, but no sisters. In other words, although there are people out there for whom their sister is the best thing that ever happened to them, I am not usually, with a few notable exceptions, friends with those people. I am drawn to those who need me as much as I need them, attracted to men and women who have not yet filled the position of sister. I have a particular chemistry with others who want to make their friends their family.

Just as I used to have nightmares that my mom was pregnant, I shudder now to think of time not spent with those beloved buddies because Laurie was along for the ride instead. Could she possibly have been all the things my friends are to me? When I get a yearning for a particular pal at a particular time, he or she comes through for me in ways that I suspect siblings wouldn't or couldn't, not without a lot of their own baggage in tow. (And friends go home, which Laurie never does.) Maybe Laurie could have a conversation with me made up entirely of Judy Blume quotes, the way Lizzy can. Maybe Laurie could gab candidly about sex after childbirth the way my steadfastly irreverent high-school posse can. Maybe, like Debbie, Laurie would have shared with me the devastation of my—*our*—father's illness, and I could have held her hand through her divorce. Maybe, instead of Debbie, Heather, and Jessica, it could have been Laurie who sat with me the night before my daughter was born, timing contractions while we awaited my husband's phone call to let us know whether *our* dad had yet emerged from his coma.

But what if she was humorless? A prude? Too chin-deep in her own grief and anxiety about our dad to be of any use? Maybe Laurie had been living out her dreams of being an actress in LA when my father's cancer was diagnosed, missing our first meeting with his oncologist because she got a walk-on role as a bimbo on *Entourage*. Maybe she was trapped at a small women's college in Georgia, a slave to the academic schedule and the pressure to publish three more articles before her tenure review when he needed to be rushed to the hospital for the fourth time in as many months.

But maybe instead of being in LA or Georgia, she was the one living downstairs from our parents when my dad was sick, giving my mom and me a break from our roles as medical escort, nurse, housekeeper, and cheerleader. After both my parents are gone, Laurie will be the only one to remember the Halloween costumes my dad sewed for me—I mean *us*—when we were little. She will remember my mom's tireless interest in entertaining us, remember how she let us wreck her hair playing beauty parlor, remember with me the stories Mom invented about the people in other cars also stuck in traffic on Friday evenings on our way up to the country. Maybe our memories of those rides in the backseat are among our most cherished.

What I know, though, is what I have. What I know is that when my dad was hours away from his last breath, it was Jessica whom I asked to find out, step-by-step, what I was supposed to do with his body when the time came. Two hours after I phoned her, she arrived at the hospital with the research neatly typed up, and sat with me in the diner across the street and wept with me into our milk shakes. And then she made me laugh by telling me about her crash course in cremation ("Why do you guys charge three times what the others charge?" she demanded of a fancy Upper East Side outfit. "Lady," the guy replied, "some people just need to pay more").

What I know is that it was my husband who moved all the paintings off the wall in the middle of the night so the stretcher could get down the stairs. Who sat with my mom in the emergency room. Who brought pictures of my dad's new granddaughter to him in the hospital to inspire him to fight the fight. Who came with my mom and me to meet with specialist after specialist to get opinion after opinion. Who stayed with my dad's body until official people came to deal, because my mom and I had to, finally, take leave of that goddamned hospital room.

Wouldn't it be good to have a sister right about now to help me cope with my dad's death? My mother's grief? To handle the estate's paperwork? To sort through seventy-five years of a magnificent and productive life? My parents have always shared me with others, but it's not a two-way street: I didn't have to share them as a kid, and I'm not about to start sharing them now. *My* dad, *my* dad's pain: He's mine, it's mine. Mine, mine, mine. Perhaps I could relieve myself of some of these new burdens if Laurie were around, but I'll never know whether she could have risen to the occasion. And so even now, one parent down, I can't bring myself to miss her. Because my parents shared me with the world, my friends became my family. Because my friends selflessly help shoulder my burdens time and time again, I can't bring myself to miss Laurie.

Most of all, it is because of my best friend that I can't bring myself to miss Laurie. Sharing a life with my husband (no tape down the middle of the bedroom) is like a giggly sleepover with Lizzy, a knee-buckling embrace at the foot of the Trevi Fountain under a starlit Roman sky, a teary milk shake with Jessica, a squabble over a shovel in the sandbox, and a sandwich hug from my parents all rolled into one, every single day. (And on the occasional day when it's not all that, there's always the café across the street for a little solo fix.) He loves me nearly unconditionally, and I feel safe, all the time. Almost as safe as I felt with my parents. And he shares me with my friends, too, just the way our—I mean *my*—parents did.

I FEEL BLESSED. I hope Laurie, wherever she may be, feels the same.

III

A SIB FOR
JUNIOR?

Parenting

A Letter to My Second Child

John Hodgman

ATTENTION UNNAMED MALE child to come:

Greetings.

Do not be alarmed. I realize you do not know who I am.

Here is a hint: You are not born yet, and already I must apologize to you.

Can you guess? My name is John Hodgman, and I am your father.

Feeling sorry, as I trust you will sadly learn, is something of a habit of mine. I am always apologizing, afraid that I have offended someone. This is because I am a person who wishes to be liked all the time. Even by hateful people. Even by historical figures I will never meet. Even by strangers and children and, naturally, by you.

Here is an example. The other day, I was at a playground with my three-year-old daughter. Surely you are familiar with my daughter? I have written about her before. In public, I refer to her as "Hodgmina."

At the playground on this spring day before you were born, Hodgmina desired to use a certain playground structure. It was a kind of corkscrew fire pole. That sounds strangely dirty, I realize. But that's what it was: a blue-painted fire pole encircled by a kind of iron corkscrew upon which children could descend in a gentle, earthbound spiral.

That sounds a little better.

According to a plaque on this structure, it was rated safe for five- to twelve-year-olds. At the moment, there were two girls circling down together, their legs entwined.

Okay. Now it sounds dirty again. But it really wasn't. They were just five-year-olds, wrapped up in each other in that unself-conscious way that children—some children—are able to achieve. Laughing, beaming, they were perfectly connected as they inched their way down.

Hodgmina and I watched them, and here I would use the adverb *sullenly*. We are both quiet people. Shy people. We do not entwine much with others. We held hands, but we were each alone. Hodgmina said quietly, "I am waiting my turn."

But I think we both knew that the older girls were never going to give her a turn. Why would they? Why should they, so perfectly mind-melded as they were in the sun and the new spring air and in their own extra-bright brilliance for coming up with this dual-corkscrew-fire-pole-riding scheme in the first place? Why should they give a turn to a younger girl on a playground in a city by a river in a world that, as far as they were concerned, did not exist?

After a period of time, I intervened. I explained that Hodgmina now wished a turn, and the older girls broke off reluctantly. Naturally, I apologized. Hodgmina walked over, and I lifted her up to the top. But I didn't let her go. I held her all the way down, guiding her fall into a slow, stuttering slide that was visibly unfun for everyone.

The structure was rated for five- to twelve-year-olds after all, and as if to explain myself to the plaque and to the world, I turned to the older girls, who were observing me skeptically. "She needs my aid," I explained, "for Hodgmina is only a three-year-old child, a little girl. She is not a big girl, like both of you."

My daughter, who has better manners than I, let this pass in silence. But believe me, when we got home, Hodgmina let me have it. Why was I apologizing to children? she asked. And why was I running her down, calling her a "little girl"? Why did I feel I had to do that?

"You're right," I said. "I'm sorry."

This is not a good habit, and I do not recommend living this way, and that is part of the reason I am writing this letter.

I AM ALSO sorry because your father, who is me, is a professional writer.

Now, don't get excited. This is a profession that often seems exciting and glamorous to young people. It did once to me as well. There was a time in my life when I, too, believed that it would be easy money to sit on beautiful lawns and write and read short stories. For reasons you will soon learn, I didn't know any better.

But to you this fact will mean mainly that your college education will be unfunded. College is where most beautiful lawns exist, of course. But you will not be able to enjoy them as I did, for you will be forced to work various menial jobs (for some reason, I picture you in a butcher's shop, trimming briskets) in order to pay for your education—all because I wanted to sit beneath a tree and read *Love in the Time of Cholera*.

Because I was something you shall never be, which is to say, an only child. I trust you shall never quite forgive us for this. But before you damn me forever, please hear this explanation.

OVER THE YEARS, many people, including your mother, who has two sisters, have asked me the same questions: What was it like to be an only child? Was it excellent? Was it better?

I would always respond the same way: "I have no idea." Just as having an elder sister will always seem innately normal to you, so being an only child was all that I had ever known. And since I had no basis for comparison, how could I possibly compare one experience to the other?

Of course, I was being polite.

The fact is, I was *always* comparing, always subjecting my siblinged peers to the cool, dispassionate analysis and reflection that only an only child has the quiet hours to cultivate, generally while watching *Doctor Who* without fear of interruption.

And my conclusion was inescapable. Being an only child was much, much better. Probably the best thing in the world.

Cast sentiment aside, and siblings are always a matter of cruel math, the unfair distribution of limited resources: cash, love, attention, patience, solitude. This is obvious on its face—even my siblinged peers knew it. That was why they asked the question in the first place.

And as they asked, I could see the quiver of dread in their eyes,

fearing an honest answer. And so I would say, "I have no idea."
Only an only child can afford such emotional generosity.

As an only child, I had gotten used to a certain lifestyle.

I was born in the Boston area in 1971, to two successful but by
no means wealthy nonwriters. My father was the eldest of three.
My mother the first of seven, though in some ways she was an only
child as well. She was older than her one brother and five sisters—
in her twenties when the last arrived (twins). And she was the first to
go to college and the only to move away from Philadelphia forever.

Did she seek for me the privacy that she had always coveted? Or
the solitude that she had always, in her own way, known? We will
never know, for she is no longer living. But by the time I was three,
the decision was made that our family would never grow larger,
and so we did the natural thing: We moved to a sixteen-room house.

Our house in leafy, nearby Brookline was the largest I have ever
been in, except for one, which I will tell you about later. It had been
a commune, but most of the surrounding homes were occupied
by attorneys and doctors and department-store heirs. And it cost
$68,000. That was real money in 1974, and not a debt my parents
took on easily. But still, that's less than five grand a room. Even at
your age, I trust you can sense a bargain.

There was a large kitchen and two pantries leading to a dining
room with a medievally massive dining-room table in it that we
dared not move. One carpeted room with a walk-in closet was, upon
closer inspection, a bathroom. From the shower to the window
seat, it was about the size of a studio apartment.

Other rooms lacked such clear identifying features, and were
more mysterious. Doors opened and opened again onto secret

staircases and massive swaths of hardwood-floored, wainscoted sunny spaces for which we had no need or purpose.

So we would wander around the house, naming the rooms. One was called, for no particular reason, "the Studio." Another was named for an old nursing colleague of my mother's who either had, or planned to, sleep there once. Occasionally in our wanderings we would bump into one of our tenants—local college students to whom we would sometimes rent a fleet of rooms out of financial need and, perhaps also, a sense of embarrassment.

But we were really alone, in the way the family of an only child is always alone. A family of three is as stable as a triangle, unlikely to collapse, each point strengthening and relying on the other. There are no favorites, no alliances but to the triangle itself. We traveled together to distant countries, saw movies together, dined together watching public television in the Studio. Even in a house in which it could take twenty-five minutes to find another soul, we were bound and insulated from the world by rooms upon rooms.

After it had lain fallow for some years, I commandeered one of these rooms for the purpose of my practicing the clarinet and the viola. This pretty much sums up being an only child to me. Only an only child could afford to take up not one but two relatively esoteric supporting instruments. And when I say afford, I speak not only of the actual cost of lessons. A siblinged child enacts his own insecurity when he picks up the guitar, the violin, the piano, those desperate showboat instruments all yearning to solo. But an only child has no need for these sorts of games. Assured of love and sustenance and space and time, the only child is free to cultivate idiosyncrasy.

And I cultivated it ruthlessly. I grew my hair long. I wore cowboy shirts and jumpsuits and I carried a briefcase. I wore a fedora.

Yes, on top of the long hair. Rightly, my grade-school peers saw me as a kind of space alien. Perhaps, my unnamed child, this is what you think I am trying to save you from. This isolation and poor fashion sense. But no, I am telling you, this was the best.

By the time I was entering high school, our last tenant had left, and I inherited a suite of rooms as large as our current apartment. I had a bedroom, a bathroom, and a living room furnished from scavenged castoffs. My bunk beds (yes, I had bunk beds! Why not? Why not tribeds? Only my imagination limited the perverse excess!) were broken apart and arranged into an L-shaped sofa; a green shaded lamp lit a manual typewriter on which I would write letters and short stories. I had a tall fern (it was still the eighties).

An only child in a family without want is the culmination of three centuries of Enlightenment ideals: the rational, critical mind conquering want and need and the base desire to conform. A good student and an attentive son (for what did I have to prove or rebel against?) I was trusted and independent. I was a dilettante, a man of leisure, an eccentric aristocrat. Free from worldly cares, I devoted myself to my passions and hobbies: old postcards and teaching myself counterpoint. The only child in a family without want is the apex of Western civilization.

But it cannot last, of course. The apex of Western civilization cannot last, of course.

HERE IS THE story about another very large house that I promised you.

Not long ago, I visited a mansion in the mountains surrounding Aspen, Colorado.

I was in Colorado to appear as the token literary humorist at a comedy festival, and I was accompanied by a friend of mine named David, who was the token cartoonist. One evening, we were at a party surrounded by professional stand-up comedians and television personalities. I realize that this may sound very glamorous, but the fact is we were not invited to this party, and that encapsulates our whole experience in Aspen: the feeling of sitting alone, with a cartoonist, ignored, eating shrimp that were not meant for us.

As the night grew later, we began hearing chatter around us about another party to which we were not invited. Someone we did not know told us that everyone here was about to board chartered taxis to be shuttled up high into the mountains where we would enjoy the hospitality of the richest man in Aspen. We said that would be fine.

We threaded several twisting mountain roads to get there, and then our taxi slipped down a narrow driveway. And there it was: unquestionably, preposterously, the home of the wealthiest man in Aspen. It looked more like a hotel, or a modern museum: a great peaked foyer, walled with glass and elegant blond wood, the double doors open and pouring golden light upon the snow, and two turtlenecked security guards standing at the door wearing Secret Service–style earpieces.

The rest of the house was shielded by thickets of robust evergreens. We did not understand its size until we entered. It was, I would later learn, some $30 million worth of house, six floors of enormous, contemporary sleek rooms with televisions hidden in the jagged stones of the massive freestanding chimney that divided the acre of living room from the acre of dining room. There was a pool room and a private screening room and statues in the corners that sounded alarms when you got near them. There was a deck

overlooking the mountains with a massive twelve-seat outdoor dining table, and then as I looked down the deck, I noticed an identical
table some thirty feet away, and then another, going off to infinity.

The party was already churning through the house, overseen by
security guards. There seemed to be no host present. In fact he
wasn't even there.

We recognized a stagehand we had befriended. "Whose house
is this?" I asked. The stagehand answered that it was the home of a
local billionaire named Michael Goldberg, who leased private jets
and hosted John Kerry and Al Gore when they happened to be
passing through Aspen.

David asked, facetiously, if Michael Goldberg was related to the
world famous professional wrestler known only as "Goldberg."
Goldberg is not the star he once was in the wrestling world, but
you should know that he was for a time a professional wrestling
champion, the latest and most snarling and beguiling incarnation
of a long and somewhat forgotten tradition of unabashedly macho
Jewish boxers and brawlers.

"Yes!" the stagehand confirmed. "They are brothers!"

David and I got drinks and walked around, pondering this bizarre
coincidence, and then I began to notice that nestled among the
priceless paintings and sculptures there were many photographs of
Goldberg, the wrestler, in his black tights, flexing. I thought then
about the relationship these brothers must share. What affection
these titans of vastly different worlds must have for each other, but
also, what rivalry? What strange grain of competition had ground
between them, starting at birth, spurring both on to create these
ostentatious pearls . . . for one to build a palace in the mountains
and the other to become the world's most famous Jewish wrestler?

This, I realized, was not the home of an only child. This was the home of a person who from the beginning had fought for love and attention, who probably grew up having to steal food, his very sustenance, from the muscled jaws of his massive, all-consuming brother!

THE OTHER DAY, when I was in Boston, I drove by the house I grew up in. Other people live in it now. And though most things feel larger in our memory than in our real life, in this case, the house seems even larger. In part because I know that I will never be able to provide it to you or Hodgmina.

I emerged from only childhood to only adulthood, surprised to learn that life does not offer you a suite of rooms just for being alive. My wealth, instead, came early—in the confidence and assurance and limitless resources I did not have to compete for. And because I have become that most wretched of things, a professional writer, in large part seeking to recapture those lost dilettantish days, my wealth in all these things has since dwindled. In part because I was an only child, I can really only afford to have one. But yet we are taking on another, who is you.

Partly we take this leap out of hope that you will become a professional wrestler, and not just because we need some sort of retirement plan. Or if not a professional wrestler, then at least the richest man in Aspen, a mogul of the sentimental sort who has sleepovers with John Kerry and keeps a photo of his elder sister on the wall. Hodgmina may be the wrestler.

Or if not a mogul or a wrestler, then at least you may be someone who has in fact had to compete, a happy, confident person who understands from the training of childhood and not just expensive therapy that it is acceptable not to have the whole of every resource; that it is acceptable not to receive *all* the love in the world, and even to tolerate a little hate; that one does not need to explain himself to children on playgrounds or in letters.

But because I am an only child, there is another, purely selfish reason: I lost my nerve.

In 2000, my mother died of cancer, at a time when I was still childless and wracked with credit-card debt and, though married to your mother, still largely a child myself. The following year, your mother became pregnant with Hodgmina. Your mother was and is a high-school teacher in lower Manhattan. On September 10, as Hodgmina's birth approached, I interviewed a comic-book writer who was astounded that we would bring a child into the world. "This is a world of limited resources," he pointed out. We shouldn't have children just because we want them.

The next day, I watched on television as a building near your mother's school collapsed. For a few hours, I could not reach her and did not know where she was, or what would happen next. Suddenly, solitude seemed about to return in the worst way possible. I flashed briefly on a life in mourning: me and a fern, alone again, and it was not anything I wanted anymore. And then the phone rang.

On balance, these hard experiences were perfectly ordinary, hardly as sad as others endured and still endure. But I understood suddenly that I was susceptible to fate in ways others are not. My parents had a similar realization, I think, when I left home to go to college, immediately got drunk, and fell down a tall staircase. "What if you had died?" my mother asked by phone when I explained why they would be getting an ambulance bill. They learned then, as I did later, that there is indeed a way for a triangle to suddenly collapse, and what is left when it does is nothing at all. My mother, contemplating this, wondered aloud, "Did we do something wrong?"

"No," I said. "You did everything right. I am sorry." I am sorry. I am sorry.

And so you see, I cannot take the risk. Like a farmer who needs children to till the soil and cannot risk having but one, so I need more than one child to lower my risk of absolute awful heartache.

To be honest, I do not know how this will work out. I, the only child, find it difficult to understand how love can be dispersed between two children. And there will be other shortages. There will be no perfect triangle. There will be alliances and counteralliances. There will be no short stories written near a fern. The stories that you write will be those you conspire out of nighttime conversation with Hodgmina. For, yes, you will live in an apartment, and you will have to share a room.

But you will be freer to fail, as your errors will be outshadowed by Hodgmina's and vice versa. And thus you will free yourselves of the unfair burden to avoid death at all costs. And maybe this is not entirely selfish. By having you, unnamed male child, I have chosen to give you both less so that at the end, as point by point of the shape of our family disappears, you will not have lost everything.

I hope when that time comes you will remember this letter and feel that I have nothing to apologize for. But just in case: I am sorry.

That is all.

John Hodgman

My Jane

Peter Ho Davies

M Y SON, OUR first child, is just about to turn nine months old as I write this and already, even before the dark circles of sleeplessness have begun to fade, friends are asking my wife and me if we're going to have another. I tend to let my wife answer for us, invariably in the negative, though depending on her mood the answer might take the form of a crisp "no," an ironically inflected "I don't think so?", even once a positively Churchillian "Nev-ah." The *tone* of her answer has a lot to do with the kind of day we're having, as our friends understand. The older ones tell us not to be so sure, we might change our minds. "Give it time," they say, patting our hands. But the *substance* of our demurrals is precisely that we have no time to give. Even if we wanted another child, my wife bumped up against that chill clinical phrase "advanced maternal age" once too often during her pregnancy.

On the surface, I don't bridle at the question as much as my

wife, goaded twice over by the reminder of her age and the linger-
ing social expectation of what she *should* want (babies, and more
babies). It's meant as a compliment, I tell her, this question of "another," a compliment to our baby—*He's so lovely, who wouldn't
want another?*—but secretly I can't help feeling a small twinge of
hurt on his part—*Isn't he enough?*—as if, our interrogators are
suggesting that he needs a sibling to complete him somehow, as
if, along with the best crib, car seat, and toys we can afford, we owe
him this. As if only childhood is a deprivation.

Of course, this twinge is because I'm an only child myself. The
truth is I let my wife answer our friends' inquiries about that fictional future child not because it's her body, not because she's the
"expert" on babies, but because she's one of four kids. Somehow, for
me to declare that my son's going to be an only, like myself, smacks
of . . . self-interest, self-regard, selfishness—the very "spoiled" qualities only children are stereotypically assigned. And, if I'm being
honest, it *is* a little of all of those. I've liked being an only child, enjoyed all the advantages of singular attention. Now, though, as my
parents grow older, I'm becoming aware of the solitary responsibility that this entails, and, since my son's arrival, I've also been
thinking of what lies before him, casting my mind back to my
early childhood, when being an only child did feel at times like a
kind of poverty, when I used to nag my mother, pull at her hem,
begging for a sibling, exactly as I used to wheedle for a new toy.

I was good at it, too—the wheedling—in a coolly calculating
way, and nearly always got what I wanted. I *was* a spoiled only child,
after all. But on this one thing, this desire for a sibling, my mother
always stood fast, and it seems to me now that perhaps I—and
maybe all only children—was so spoiled precisely to make up for

this one withheld boon. My Welsh father was one of three, and my Chinese mother one of a brood so large that she seemed to have siblings to spare—one even sent back to the family in China before my mother was born—so extended that her siblings seemed at either end of the age spectrum to merge with parents and grand-parents, nephews and nieces. What must it have been like for my parents to imagine my childhood, alone? And yet, even as they spoiled me to make up for it, they never had another child, and when I asked my mother recently she told me why: "You were such a difficult baby!" So there it is. It was my own fault.

Thankfully, I never understood that as a child. And I kept up my asking, pleading, perhaps as late as the age of ten. "How do you even know you want a brother or sister?" my mother would ask, pointing out reasonably enough that I could hardly miss what I'd never had. But, I could, of course, because what I'd never had was present all around me, in the parallel lives of school friends and cousins, but even more intimately and pervasively in the TV shows and, particularly, books of my youth. I learned to read with a pair of siblings, Peter and Jane (the British counterparts of Dick and Jane), and, not surprisingly, I grew up wondering where my Jane was. When I graduated at seven or eight to what we'd now call young-adult books, it was another Peter, a character in the Enid Blyton Secret Seven series of children's mysteries, that I identified with. And he, too, had a sister named . . . *Janet*. Mere coincidence? Or, as the Secret Seven's preteen sleuths would be quick to suspect, a *clue*?

In such adventures, and Blyton's other popular series, the Famous Five, only children—in my recollection, at least—always felt like outsiders. If not actually villains, they were often weak, hangers-on, never the rescuers but frequently in need of rescue. True, only children weren't as badly off as the orphans of children's literature, yet orphans at least had a kind of tragic grace, and frequently hidden reserves of pluck, or special compensatory talents.

What all those Blyton books made me feel most, I think, was that to have siblings was to be normal. All kids may want to be normal, but as a mixed-race child in predominantly white middle-class Britain in the 1970s, I wanted it more than most. The two other Asian kids I knew in school, both boys—one half Filipino, the other Jamaican-Chinese—were also coincidentally only children. Is it any wonder I confused the stigmas? Any wonder that I yearned to be part of one of Blyton's very English, very white clubs? If I couldn't change the way I looked, I must have reasoned, I could at least have a sibling. I shrink in shame from this thought now, but perhaps what I was really asking my mother when I pleaded for a sibling was not to give me an ally, a second, but somehow magically to make *me* again.

SHE NEVER GAVE in to my pleas, and in the continuing absence of a sibling, I found myself drawn back over and over again to those Blyton stories, for the vicarious thrill of siblings, until the very works that provoked my desire for brothers and sisters began to slake it, too. I devoured those Secret Seven books (that the Famous Five were actually four plus a dog rather offended my eight-year-old sensibility), the whole series of them, each written according to the same formula—a mysterious but petty crime solved by intrepid child sleuths, followed by cake or ice-cream rewards, and much hip-hip-hooraying. In retrospect, the adventures themselves were forgettable—though the residual memory of the cheery middle-class pluck of Blyton's characters is, I suspect, one of the nostalgic pleasure that draws so many British adults to the Harry Potter books that ape it—but in their very formulaic repetition there was clearly some essential comfort, as if each new book was a member of the same family, the same basic features with minor variations, as if each book was essentially a sibling to the last. That's perhaps the same pleasure we take in any new offering from an author we love, discerning the family nose, or smile, beneath the fake beard or fresh makeup of the new work. At any rate, it was a small step for me from a series of books about siblings to the whole extended family of literature.

If my desire for a sibling was truly an expression of a desire to become another, fiction was a perfect outlet. Books and reading swiftly came to fill that space, provide that special intimacy (which, among other things, excluded parents) that I imagined siblings did for others. There must have come some point, however, when I began to stop seeing the heroes of stories as siblings, as figures of identification, and began instead to transfer that allegiance to their authors.

It's an uncharted point, to be sure, lost in the past of my reading, and probably buried, too, under the sheer weight of embarrassment all writers feel toward their juvenilia. All I can recall now is some early scribbled fantasy, not of a new addition to the family, but an old one—a long-lost elder brother or sister, run away from home precisely because they didn't have siblings; *ha!*—who I, in a precocious irony, had been meant to replace, and who might any day now return home to find me and decide to stay—*hip-hip-hooray!*—to the overwhelming gratitude of my chastened parents.

Such childish imaginings aside, the notion of the author as a

kind of sibling to the reader still feels persuasive to me. It's a connection I'd like to imagine as so intimate it approaches a kind of
ESP (as in my idealized image of siblings), but with none of the
connotations of a romantic relationship. The first modern short
story, after all—Gogol's "The Overcoat"—contains as its signal
emotional moment a second of recognition when one nameless
young clerk looks across his office at Akaky Akakievich, the down-
trodden comic hero, and empathizes with him, in these words: "I
am your brother." It's arguably the first epiphany in modern literature, the spark that sets the fire of all the short stories to follow,
and it's the recognition of a (metaphorical) sibling.

I WAS REMINDED of all this recently, while looking in a local
bookstore for something new to read to my son. I'd drifted from
the shelves of blanketlike soft books to the reassuringly blockish
board books, drawn, as if into the future, to the young-adult section to see if I recognized any of the titles. I didn't, and after a mild
pang that there were none of Blyton's books on the shelves I felt a
kind of hopeful reassurance that perhaps my son—born in a time
when only children seem much more common—might not feel
so in need of siblings, whether real or fictional.

Heading back to the baby-book shelves, I saw a glossy volume
of fairy tales, and on its cover there was an illustration from *Cinderella,* the one story I suddenly recalled that had made me re-
lieved to be an only child, not subject to the tyranny of (step)siblings.
But even as I reached for the book, its picture of the prince kneeling, glass slipper in one hand, Cinderella's foot raised in the other,
reminded me of another story altogether, Flannery O'Connor's famous and famously bitter short story "A Good Man Is Hard to

Find," the climax of which memorably features the seduction of a girl by a traveling Bible salesman (the marvelously named Manley Pointer) who perversely makes off not with her virginity but with her artificial leg (it's the South; what can I say?). I've taught the story in literature and creative writing classes for years—it's a staple of anthologies—but for the first time it seemed to me that its climax represents a kind of ironic, even dyspeptic, reversal of the Cinderella story, the young man grasping the leg not to try on a slipper but to make off with it whole. Now, I should say, I've no idea whether this was really O'Connor's intention or not. I'm no scholar of her work, and I've never come across such an interpretation in my peripatetic reading of the criticism. Still, a few other textual clues (the existence of a pair of pseudo stepsisters—beautiful, rather than ugly in this case—nicknamed Glycerin and Caramel, say) might support it. And, of course, I *want* to believe it. The insight just feels right, feels, indeed, like an inspiration—one that was first the author's, then, belatedly, mine, the reader's. And behind the revelatory force of this new recognition was the possibility that other readers (like myself on countless past readings) had missed the echo. Part of my pleasure, then, in the insight was the feeling that I'd been singled out by it; the sense that the story was suddenly speaking to me alone.

All reading operates like this to an extent. A book, unlike a movie or a TV show, is consumed one individual at a time, its impact unaffected by how many other people may have read it, or whether others are enjoying it with you. But it had never struck me so powerfully how the intimacy of reading, of the connection between author and reader, relies on the possible exclusion of other readers. But, surely, that's what intimacy is: not closeness alone, but the feeling of being closer to someone than anyone else. And there in that bookstore, surrounded by children's books, it seemed to me that this is what I've always looked for in my reading, an intimacy that in that moment, at least, felt like my ideal of a sibling relationship. It was as if I'd found, in Flannery O'Connor (of all people!) a long-lost sibling—my Jane—whispering to me in the dark, after our parents had turned out the lights.

I bought that book of fairy tales for my son, of course. I'll read them to him until he can read them with me. He'll enjoy them, I hope, but I bought them for myself as much as for him, to remind me that however the times may have changed, whatever the remaining, and hopefully dwindling, stigma attached to being an only child, he'll still need to find those inspired connections to others (others who won't, can't, be me or his mother), that epiphanic sense of recognition across a crowded room, or through pages of type: *I am your brother.*

Incidentally, before I left the store, I also bought a new copy of Flannery O'Connor's collected works, not for my son—he'll find his own literary siblings, not of my choosing—but for my mother, I think, to show her that all my begging was not in vain, after all.

SUCCUMBING TO TWO

AMY RICHARDS

O UR EXPERIENCES AND memories of our families are emotional as well as tangible, but the tangible does not always dictate what the emotional will be. The power of suggestion is palpable.

In early adolescence, when asked if I had any siblings, I replied, "No, I'm a lonely child." The irony was this: I actually loved being an only child. Not only did I never feel the absence of siblings, I never felt alone. I had friends—real and imaginary, peers and adults—to entertain me. I spent the majority of my childhood in Williamsport, Pennsylvania, where I lived in a double house with two brothers next door. It was the early seventies and my neighborhood was chock-full of tykes. I stayed out until sundown playing kickball, trading baseball cards, riding my bike. Nothing— other than the fact that I had my own room—seemed to indicate that I was different from my neighborhood pals, all of whom had siblings.

Nonetheless, at a young, impressionable age, I bought into the stereotype that only children are lonely children. My genuine respect for my family and my positive, legitimate feelings about them were often overshadowed by this societal assumption that my family was "incomplete" because there was only one of me. If there is only one, there must be a reason: a messy divorce, infertility, or just general instability. The status quo is simply that you *should* have more than one. People made presumptuous comments like "But, *why* don't you have siblings?" or, pityingly, "You can come to *my* house." Externally, I went along. Internally, I knew better.

Only children get bad press. I did have friends, fellow onlies, who confessed to feeling lonely, thus legitimizing the image. But friends with siblings were lonely, too, suggesting that these feelings of isolation were not directly linked to an absence of sisters and brothers. It depends on how you situate yourself and how much responsibility you take for creating your community. I still have adult friends who depend on others to take the initiative to make plans. Rather than extend themselves, they wallow in self-pity. Their loneliness is of their own making.

What is, and what is believed to be, are often at odds. I am the only child of a single mother. I never knew my father. My mother left him two months before I was born on the premise that he was crazy. Years later she was proved correct when he was arrested for kidnapping an adolescent male patient after running a successful psychiatric practice, though he was not a licensed psychiatrist. No matter how many times I clarify the details of this story, people continue to assume that it was my mother and I who were abandoned.

As the single child of a single mother, I had more of everything: more opportunities, more chores, more access, more responsibility, and more attention. For better or worse, there was no mediator to negotiate our parent-child drama, no one else to parcel things out to, no one to share the blame for the broken window, no one to fight with over Mom's generosity, no one to share the burden of her bad moods. But neither was there anyone to be compared to or compete with. I was frequently left to my own devices and became a pro at entertaining myself, gaining a tremendous sense of independence early on. Part of that independence was uniquely mine, and part was encouraged by my young mother. I never knew the kids' table. I expected to have a say in how our house was decorated or what kind of car we were going to buy. Though at age eight I was hardly a financial contributor to our household, I felt equal ownership. I was treated—and acted—like an adult.

It's easy to romanticize this childhood, especially within the context of my current career as a feminist writer and activist: My mother is a heroine. She ditched that louse, struck out on her own, put herself through college, got increasingly better jobs, sent me on fancy vacations and to private schools, and raised me to take initiative and to see obstacles as something to be surmounted. She didn't *need* a man. She triumphed over the patriarchy; long live the matriarchy. This perspective is, of course, in hindsight and slightly exaggerated. But convention really isn't in everyone's best interest. I know many people who weren't served by being part of a standard nuclear family. It works for some, but can't be mandated for all.

But the truth, at least from my mother's perspective, is that she wouldn't have done it alone if she didn't have to. She would have preferred to have raised me with the help of a partner. Yet I wasn't raised alone. I had an exceptionally supportive grandfather and aunt—as the African proverb (and Hillary Clinton) maintain, it takes a village. For me, the most punishing aspect of having a single working parent was that my mother could rarely drive carpool. A small price to pay for the unique partnership my mother and I shared.

Living in the moment of my childhood, I never analyzed it. Time has afforded me a greater perspective on my upbringing, and while those reflections are less pure, influenced by others and by my own adult opinions, I can honestly say I loved my childhood. The only times I felt limited were when I felt insecure, perceiving myself to be different.

In college, I developed the maturity to realize that my situation was no more alternative than the nuclear family. There was no consistency among family compositions. Despite this revelation, I still had many friends who rejected their own experiences and defaulted to tradition—"I'm getting married, because we want children and it's not fair to have children out of wedlock." I also realize now that our memories of childhood derive from a feeling rather than from concrete and definitive measures. A friend once remarked that she didn't think she could ever marry someone whose parents were divorced, because that experience seemed too different from what she knew from her own family. She is now happily married to someone whose parents were divorced. I maintain that our families had more to do with their content than their form.

Besides the casual hypothesizing that I engaged in with friends about our different upbringings—was I more like the responsible older child, the attention-grabbing middle kid, the spoiled baby, an amalgamation of all, or a breed unto my own?—I didn't really give much thought to being an only child. It wasn't until friends started procreating and I contemplated creating my own family that I seriously revisited what it meant to be an only and felt compelled to examine the stereotypes anew.

Recently, a few friends who felt they wanted only one child but were afraid their inclination might be selfish and unfair called on me to defend the legitimacy of choosing to have a single child. I assured them that I was well-adjusted, not abnormally self-centered, and never resented my apparent "lack" of siblings. As proof, I shared stories of how I was often complimented with "You don't *seem* like an only child." At my eighth-grade parent-teacher conference, my teacher expressed concern to my mother because I never talked about my siblings. The teacher confessed that she had never considered that I might be an only child. I seemed too well-adjusted.

I always knew that I wanted to be a mother. And, like most everyone I know who has given serious consideration to family size, I was immediately drawn toward re-creating my own experience. Envisioning life beyond one is a challenge, yet I find myself in love with someone who is one of four and interested in re-creating *his* own experience. All I can think about is that all of the children would share one thing—the same bed, the same car seat, the same wardrobe, the same allowance, the same bicycle. Resources stretched thin. But with one, you can easily include him or her in everything. The child can go to work with you or to a friend's house for dinner, just like I did with my mother. With more than one, the fallout is likely to be an us-them scenario—parents at the dinner table, kids gone to bed. Parents in the front seat, kids in the back.

As I write this, my boyfriend and I have one child. It is still inconceivable to me that I could give a larger family the quality of life I want to provide. My primary reason for resistance is economic, but it also has to do with logistics. How could I negotiate more than one? Would I be able to stay focused on my work as a writer and an activist, most of which I do out of my apartment? Go stay with friends for the weekend the way my mom did when I was a kid? With one, sure, but two . . . that seems to be asking too much. However, it isn't really fair of me to default to comparing my situation, where there are two active and involved parents and two incomes, to my mother's more challenging experience as a single parent. Furthermore, I would be *choosing* my situation—my mother's so-called choice was a matter of survival.

I know that I have enough love for two, three, or four. But do I have the patience? And what about the opportunities that I worry I will shortchange them on? I believe in providing a comfortable quality of life. It doesn't have to be fancy, but I don't want my children to worry about health insurance or being shut out of higher education because of prohibitive costs. Like every parent, I don't want my children to suffer, and I do want the best for them. But I'm unsure if I have the financial and temporal resources to provide the best for more than one. And, based on my own experience, I am unconvinced that I would be depriving the one child I do have by not giving him siblings.

And still, despite my happy memories of being an only child, I find myself wanting more than one. Is it because of my boyfriend's inclinations? Some deep biological drive? People ask me what it's like to be one, but now I'm asking them what it's like to have two. An acquaintance recently told me she had her second child so that her older daughter would have a playmate. Other friends seem to treat childbirth and rearing like a science experiment: curiosity about what will come out next in the mix. Others are frankly invested in leaving a legacy, and most are just following the routine of life. As a feminist activist, it is my responsibility to consider the political arguments against procreating and, specifically, for limiting the number of children each woman has. I'm a white northern woman, and my children will use more natural resources than should be allowed. Because I am a white middle-class woman, no one will judge my decision to procreate—in fact, some will encourage it—but at whose expense? What about overpopulation? And how can I ignore all the children who don't have families?

Part of what is hard about succumbing to two is that I don't want that choice to be perceived as a rejection of my own happy childhood, a compromise to my boyfriend, or a capitulation to societal expectations. In the end, though, my decision is driven by sheer terror: I worry that something will happen to my child and having another would be the only thing that could get me through that. I wish there were some braver, deeper, or more theoretical underpinnings behind my ultimate motivation for two, but that's what I come up with.

Most people foster prejudices about single moms and solo children, but I, an outsider to sibling relationships, have my own judgments against the more universally accepted sibling relationship. For instance, I often feel that they are forced—why does biology trump everything? Siblings might share bedrooms and family vacations, but do they share secrets and values? Sometimes, but not always. Do people turn to their siblings in their moment of need or to share their favorite experiences? Some, but not all. Do we know a brother or a sister better or even as well as we know our friends? Do we know (or even care about) their likes and dislikes, their most embarrassing moment, their favorite vacation spot? People are fiercely loyal to their siblings, but the motivation, while primal, is still a mystery to me. Why, with all of the documentation of different family scenarios, do we revert to defining family in conventional terms? We have been able to expand our definition of "family" to include stepfamily, adopted siblings, and so on, but can we go one step further and drain biology from the requirements of family? Can't family truly be chosen? Why don't we leave more space for the emotional relationships that often sustain us better than the blood ones?

As I contemplate depriving my child of the riches of onlyhood, these questions linger. Just as I had to defy societal assumptions about only children, my current challenge is to rise above my own bias toward and pride in the *nonlonely* onlies and embrace the possibility of becoming a mother of two.

MOTHER OF TWO

JANICE P. NIMURA

ATURDAY NIGHT, eight o'clock. One-year-old David is asleep early for once, and almost-four Clare in her pink pajamas is in the living room with us. Not quite bedtime for her, not yet. It's quiet, toys put away, dishwasher whooshing behind the closed kitchen door.

I've got some reading in my lap and a red pen in my hand, which intrigues her—why do I get to write in my book, when she's not supposed to write in any of hers? I'm underlining the important words, I explain, so that I'll remember them later. It's something grown-ups get to do when they're working.

She disappears, then returns with a red pen and a section of the newspaper, throws herself belly down next to me on the rug.

"What are you doing?" I ask.

"Working," she answers, carefully underlining one word, then another. "I'm finding all the words with c's in them. What's this one say?"

"'Church.'"

"What's this one?"

"'Choreographer.'"

"What's that mean?"

"Someone who makes up dances."

"I do that sometimes!"

Yoji puts down his magazine and joins her on the floor. The two of them become engrossed in the national weather map, which is soon covered with ballpoint dots.

"This is where I grew up"—dot in the vicinity of Seattle—"and here is where you're growing up, in New York."

"Where did Mommy grow up?"

"In New York, just like you."

We play this game till bedtime, trying to come up with friends outside the tristate area, which is getting too crowded with dots. Sweet, calm time. So this is what it must feel like to have an only child.

Four of Clare's preschool classmates are only children. I'm always thinking about how straightforward their parents' lives must be now that everyone's turning four. One bedtime. One bath. One appetite to consider at each meal. One set of instructions for the babysitter. One folding cot in the corner of a hotel room. One small voice in the night. Four-year-olds sleep well, on average; they eat what adults eat, for the most part; they are capable of entertaining themselves in a car. They can reason, and though it's sometimes hard to tell, they really do know the right thing to do if they stop and think about it.

· · ·

DAVID PLOWS INTO Clare's block tower and one of the blocks clips her on the chin. She picks it up and throws it at him. When they both scream at the same time the sound is almost visible. There is fault on both sides, but aggression trumps accident, and Clare needs to apologize. When there's only one parent home it takes longer—pick David up and Clare shrieks, "That's *my* lap," put David down and he wails like an ambulance. We're still fairly far from anything resembling a "Sorry, David" when my mother calls. "Man," I say to her over the noise, "you had it *easy*."

To hear my mother tell it, I was a model specimen. I threw tantrums only during the age range when Dr. Spock said to expect them. I slept well, on average. I ate well, for the most part. I wore what my mother chose for me. Later on I did well in school, liked books and my teachers. I shook hands firmly, enjoyed the company of adults, thrived on praise, knew my limits. Instead of moving to a larger apartment when I was born, my parents bought the railroad flat above us and put in a spiral staircase. I slept upstairs in what was essentially my own little apartment, complete with a door out to the elevator landing. I never sneaked out, not once. I don't think it occurred to me. I was incapable of subterfuge. One afternoon in middle school a friend and I went to an R-rated movie. *St. Elmo's Fire*, I think it was. Rob Lowe having sex! I confessed to my mother by dinnertime.

I grew up happy, secure, and totally dependent on adult approval. In our family of three I was always going to be outnumbered, so I never put up a fight. Most of the time, I just assumed my parents were right. (Most of the time, in hindsight, they were.) Making up my own rules would have been too scary. I did what I was told, and that was fine, if a little limited. I never tried to negotiate; I might mutter dark imprecations under my breath, but I never dared tell anyone off. After school one day I watched a friend call her mother a jerk to her face; I remember physically cringing as I waited for the lightning to strike. I didn't just tolerate authority, I needed it. I hated working in groups, hated sharing a cabin with nine other girls at summer camp—any situation when the inmates seemed to be running the asylum.

OVER BREAKFAST YOJI explains to Clare what "only child" means. Intrigued by her response to this, I ask which she thinks is more fun, Only Childhood or Big Sisterdom.

"Big sister," she answers without hesitation.

"Why?"

"You get to do more."

"More what?"

She considers this. "More things."

"Like what?"

"Like . . . like play ring-around-the-rosy."

And there it is, elegant as a zen koan. She has someone nearly her size to sleep next to, eat next to, join hands and dance with. Someone who's not a parent or a teacher, not someone to please but just someone to play with, scheme with, misbehave with. And fight with. I never learned how to have a good fight, never understood how you could really mix it up with someone without killing a friendship, not until I'd been married quite a while. I'm still not good at it.

Clare and David are already pros. Clare's voice rises fiercely from the living room: "*No,* David, I don't *like* it when you do that!"

Sound of treasure (doll, crayon, truck) being yanked out of David's fist, then David's shriek of fury. Five minutes later they're taking turns putting LEGO blocks on each other's heads and giggling helplessly as they watch them tumble off.

WHEN I WAS little, no one ever grabbed my toys. My upstairs nest was always just the way I wanted it, books lined up neatly, Monopoly and Sorry! and Parcheesi stacked above them, china animals in a row. We never moved, so there was never a reason to weed out or update. A mirror eventually replaced the picture of Raggedy Ann over the dresser; my bed shifted from one wall to another. But the bed was the same, painted red with a trundle underneath for sleepovers, and the dresser had been my changing table when I was born. Anne of Green Gables and Laura Ingalls Wilder and Mrs. Piggle-Wiggle came down from their shelf to be reread regularly. My room had odd skinny double doors that didn't close properly, but it didn't matter—there was no one to bar them against. I rarely even shut them.

I liked having friends over, but I liked it when they left, too. You can't sit down and read a book in the middle of a playdate. (I had a solution for that one, though: When we played house, I pretended to be the teenage babysitter who had to do her homework after the kids were in bed.) Being alone was my balm and my tonic; I needed it as much as sleep.

Yoji traces my shortcomings as a team player to my lack of siblings—my idea of teamwork, he says, is "Okay, everyone go off and do your part of the job and meet back here when you're done." He's right. To me, "If you want it done right, do it yourself" sounds like common sense, not compulsiveness. It's much easier to become a control freak when there are no little brothers around to topple your block towers. I like things to run on time, to go according to plan. I'm always five minutes early. I get crabby when it's time to go and I'm the only one who's ready. I'm extremely reliable, and more than a little rigid. Though with two children in the house, that is changing. As Clare says, "When you have a little brother, you have to be flexible."

I was an unusually "only" only child. My father was an only child, and my mother might as well have been—her sister was six years younger, only ten when my mother left for college. I was the only grandchild on both sides, no cousins at all. Yoji's brother, older by four years, used to handcuff him to chairs and goad him into sticking his fingers in electrical sockets. ("Never liked the way that felt," he says, shuddering.) Every day contained the possibility of both unexpected danger and the exhilaration of running with the big kids. It made him flexible, and it made him game.

CLARE AND DAVID and I set out for Central Park while the June day is still relatively cool. David starts his morning nap in the stroller, and Clare and I pick up doughnuts from the coffee cart on the corner. We're lucky this morning—they still have our favorite ones: plain for me, sugar for her. We also get a raisin bagel for David when he wakes up. Parking the stroller in the shade, we spread a blanket on Cedar Hill and munch contentedly, looking for ants and four-leaf clovers and trying to spot the cardinals we can hear trilling in the trees.

"Look, Mommy, crispy clouds," she says, pointing.

"D'you mean wispy?"

"Yeah, wispy clouds. And a helicopter!"

David opens his eyes and smiles at the doughnuts. Clare jumps up—"David's awake!"—and tries to unbuckle the stroller straps. Soon they're moving away across the grass together, Clare walking slowly so as not to outpace David, who crawls at her heel like a dog. They plant themselves a few yards apart and start tossing a ball back and forth, grinning at each other.

It seems to me that a sibling, if you're lucky, is the first and most lasting experience of emotional intimacy with a peer. An only child has friendships, but friends have to be chosen and cultivated and kept up with. They change over time. I am lucky in my friendships, a healthy handful of which date all the way back to kindergarten. But I never had a "best friend," the kind you talk to every other day, who knows your goals and your secret fears. The kind you trust completely. It wasn't until the first semester of college that I found one, someone I stayed up till all hours with just talking, someone to whom I gave complete access to everything I thought and felt. I ended up marrying him.

Yoji knows me better than anyone in the world. But he doesn't know how the light glowed yellow through the shutters on my bedroom window in the morning, or what it felt like to lock myself in the upstairs bathroom and hum with my hands over my ears, trying to shut out the sound of a rare argument from my parents' bedroom below. He doesn't know me all the way back to the beginning.

A sibling relationship isn't built; it just grows, from the beginning. Clare can't remember a time before David. They share a room and a rhythm. They rub off on each other. She is self-contained and acutely observant, and he is a cuddly clown; she has taught him which buttons to push on the stereo, and he has taught her how to hug. She holds him in front of her to go down the tall spiral slide at the playground, and at the bottom they're both beaming with pride.

One night David throws up in his crib. Clare watches with wide eyes as we set to work with damp paper towels and fresh sheets, then darts out of the room. Minutes later she is back, having wrestled open the refrigerator door, found a sippy cup, and filled it with cold water from the pitcher. David is shivering and crying, but quiets when she hands him the cup. At four, she already knows how to help him feel better. And he already looks to her for comfort.

I HAD PLENTY of friends growing up, but inside my head the relationships were often a little fraught. Is she *really* my friend? Or would she actually rather be spending time with someone else? Part of this was a girl thing—girls are mean in their own special way, and I went to an all-girls school, without the mitigating presence of brothers at home. In third grade someone left an anonymous note in my locker: "Alex G. doesn't really like you. She really hates you." But part of it was me. A more socially confident kid would have thrown that note away and pitied its author. I put it in my pocket and let it fester. Decades later, as we pushed our strollers together in the park, I asked Alex if she remembered the note. She looked blank. And somewhere inside of me, an eight-year-old finally relaxed.

In high school I felt as if I had somehow missed the week where they taught us about clothes and boys and what to do on Saturday nights. Suddenly these girls I'd known forever seemed to speak a language I hadn't learned. They went shopping in SoHo and bought fake IDs on Fourteenth Street and smoked at the coffee shop across the street from school. On weekends, they Went Out. I babysat.

I turned out okay. The end of adolescence was the end of most of my self-doubt. At college I discovered that boys didn't torture one another the way girls could. I spent so much time with Yoji and his refreshingly uncatty roommates that my mother started calling us Wendy and the Lost Boys. But before that I had wasted a lot of time second-guessing myself, picking the scabs of embarrassing moments that no one else had noticed.

Back in the park, watching Clare and David toss their ball, I know this scene—blue sky, green grass, two dark-haired, dark-eyed, apple-cheeked children—will be one that won't fade. It captures everything I strive for as a parent: a girl and a boy who each have, as I did, all the unhurried attention from their parents, all the opportunity for individualness they need; a sister and a brother who rejoice in each other's existence, and draw from it another kind of strength, one that I am just beginning to understand.

BATHTIME. CLARE IS herding bubbles toward her end of the tub. David is sucking on a washcloth and pouring water over the side. Their fingers and toes are wrinkled like prunes.

"Time to get out," I decide, brandishing towels.

"We don't want to get out," Clare retorts. "Do we, David?" He grins at her, and goes back to his washcloth.

Solidarity. David's not even talking yet, and they're already in league. Won't be long before we'll hear them whispering about us after lights-out.

I find that thrilling.

MINORITY REPORT

JUDITH THURMAN

A TRIANGLE IS the most stable geometric form, except, perhaps, in the case of two parents and an only child. Only children are, by definition, underdogs—a minority of one—and at the same time, they have too much clout and significance: the redemptive power, or so they imagine, to repair what is broken and fill what is empty in their parents' lives. The necessity to rise and shine daily, like a puny sun around which two mighty satellites revolve, nurtures a grandiose and morbid perfectionism, which can, however, like the training in solitary confinement one gets from an only childhood, be useful to a writer.

NEITHER OF MY parents was an only child. My father had eight siblings; my mother, three. They were both depressives, or, rather, my mother was a depressive and my father was depressed—she because of her chemistry, he because he gave up a profession he loved, the law, to go to war, in 1943, and afterward took an unrelated job he hated, and they moved to a suburb where they had no roots, no car, no attachments, no recreations, and nothing in common with their more materially ambitious neighbors. Only children lack the perspective—the sense of reality, which is to say, of relativity—provided by a personal history with multiple narrators, allies, rivals, and witnesses, hence alternate plots. Depression, the overcast weather of our nuclear family life, which rarely lifted, was the climate of normality to me. I didn't realize it wasn't normal— that there was, in fact, no normality, and no uniqueness, either— until, at sixteen, I left home.

I AM A late-born only child who is now the mother of a late-born child—a sixteen-year-old son who was the only child of both parents (his father is a late-born only, too) until his half sister arrived, ten years ago. They tussle with, tease, protect, and love each other, but grew up a continent apart, and are, in some ways, more like cousins than siblings. I call my son's sister—and think of her as— my "niece," but we need some new kinship designations (horizontal, not hierarchical) to keep up with the evolution of family life. My current partner, for example (an only child, of course), has an only daughter of twenty-two, and I would like to find an honorific that expresses a uniquely fond, complicitous rapport enriching to both of us. There isn't one. Conventional genealogical trees allow step and half relatives their branches—but what of the chicks who nest in them?

In my youth, I couldn't see myself mothering a brood, even of two, although I am now sorry that my maternal ambition—and imagination—was so limited. My childhood friends, for the most part, married young and reproduced at a normal age for our

generation, and thus became adults in their twenties or early thirties, fully loaded with mortgages, insurance, and steady jobs, while
I prolonged a grasshopper's life—unsettled and bohemian—until
the term of my pregnancy, at forty-two. Though I envied their substance, they envied my lightness. I eagerly accepted, however, the
intermittent and mostly delightful responsibility of becoming a
godmother eight times over (the youngest of my spiritual nurslings
is nine, the oldest thirty-five), and I have also managed to acquire—
as only children tend to—a large, extended family of siblings by
affinity. Our intimacy has been tested over the years by various
forms of adversity, though not the primal ones that brothers and
sisters encounter growing up (having to withstand jealousy and
comparison; sharing a bedroom, a backseat, dirty secrets, and love),
or the burdens that fall to the middle-aged offspring of elderly, widowed, or incapacitated parents, followed by the fruits or headaches
of an estate. An only child is a sole inheritor in every sense.

IN REREADING THIS brief musing, I found a stylistic inconsis-
tency that I was going to revise, but decided (with atypical toler-
ance for my lapses) to flag instead. In one sentence, I repudiate the
existence of "normality" and "uniqueness"—not only as an only
child, but as a human being—yet elsewhere, I casually and unself-
consciously use both terms. A biographer discovers that embedded in most lives, especially literary ones, there is a dialectical
principle—two poles with an opposite charge that behave like a
force field, shaping a subject's sense of self and view of the
world. In the case of Isak Dinesen, those poles were Kierkegaard's
Either/Or, the aesthetic and the moral imperatives. In the case of
Colette, they were the Pure and the Impure—categories that

helped her understand her culture's too strictly assigned notions of gender; the ambiguities of self-exposure and concealment in her writing; and the condition of an inveterately needy woman who, just as inveterately, yearned for autonomy. In my own case, and perhaps for many only children, those antipodes are "normality" and "uniqueness," the former an unfamiliar state that one idealizes, yet also obscurely mistrusts and disdains; the latter a neat description of the predicament and privilege of being the lone egg in the basket.

IV

STILL ONLY AFTER

ALL THESE YEARS

Tables Turned

THE FOREST OF MEMORY

KATHRYN HARRISON

A S A GIRL contemplating the mysteries and attractions of independence, of growing up and moving away from home to attend college and then graduate school—moving toward what I believed would be my real, or real*er*, life—I never imagined myself entering the world of adults as an *only child*. Wasn't this a state of being that ended, necessarily, with childhood? After all, no one spoke of "only adults." As far as I could tell, unattached adults included the not-yet-married who were looking for love, single mothers or fathers who'd perhaps given up on love, divorcées on the rebound, people confirmed in spinsterhood or bachelordom, and those who had married and were subsequently widowed. My mother, once an only child, solved the problem of motherhood by leaving me with her parents and was now no longer "only" but "single." In the wake of my father's departure she'd had a handful of affairs and, by the time I was ten, had embarked on the one that would become her last, with a man who left (but did not divorce) his devoutly Catholic wife to live with my mother, at whose side he remained until her death, from cancer, at forty-three. Long before I had the ability to articulate the observation, I understood that the aloneness of adults was measured in terms of romantic coupling. The term for it—the state of being "single"—sounded enough like "singular" to seem desirable to me. Certainly it was a much more attractive word than "only," with its connotations of meagerness, of deprivation, its annoying habit of rhyming with "lonely."

I was born in 1961 and raised among families in which not only single parents but also single children were very much an exception to the nuclear rule; all of my peers seemed to have at least one brother or sister. The worst of being an only child, I felt, was the pity it elicited from those adults who seemed to assume that I lacked what they considered a genuine childhood. Was this undertaking impossible in the absence of siblings? A family of seven lived next door to my grandparents, and whenever I liked I could sample their noise and chaos and petulant squabbling and then escape when I'd had my fill of what struck me as a more uncomfortably Darwinian existence than my own.

By virtue of being middle-aged I am no longer an only child. At least I don't call myself one, not any more than I began to identify myself as an orphan after my grandmother's death left me, at the age of thirty, the single living member of my original family. Unencumbered by primary relations, neither do I have any aunts, uncles, or cousins, because my mother had no siblings and my father was gone by the time I turned one. Whether or not I admit to being an only child, I am, unarguably, the sole keeper of my early history.

Who else would care to preserve my bronzed baby shoes, my

christening dress, or my grade-school report cards? Who else will inherit my mother's baby teeth, my grandfather's reading glasses, my grandmother's purse, in it her wallet filled with expired credit cards, many for businesses that no longer exist? My great-grandfather's Masonic ring. A silver baby rattle, blackened by tarnish—whose? A tiny Torah scroll wound inside a sterling, filigreed ark, and (in the same lockbox, hidden in one envelope sealed inside another) an antique gold pendant in the form of a swastika, that ancient cosmic symbol that before 1935 had yet to become an object of terror and loathing. A crystal goblet commemorating the coronation of Edward VIII on May 12, 1937. Three canes that once belonged to my grandfather (one unscrews to reveal a hidden dagger, the weapon of a gentleman who walked alone, at night, in dangerous cities). A pair of very beautiful hardwood shoe trees (also his). And hundreds of photographs, some of people I no longer recognize, if I ever did, many taken decades before I was born. I could go on and on, boring even myself, because the entire inventory of my family's "material history," as an anthropologist would call such a collection, belongs to me. It is mine to do with what I will, to make sense of, perhaps, assembling the pieces into a coherent whole, a kind of narrative group portrait complete with background and foreground. Or to make into fiction, to invent a history that is possible, but untrue.

That swastika, to take the most dramatic, and puzzling, example: Where, and from whom, did my Jewish grandmother acquire such an object? Why did she keep it? Her only sibling, an older sister who lived in Paris, barely survived the German occupation. Wrapped up as the gold swastika is, hidden for the shameful thing it has become, upon such a piece of evidence I could begin to fabricate a sinister relative, a diseased branch on my family tree. Like all the contents of those boxes stacked in my basement, the swastika is solid, immutable. No, this is not true: A fire could melt it down, consign it to the same fate as that of gold fillings pried from the teeth of those who weren't, like my great-aunt, saved by a Christian friend. Still, if it isn't immutable, the gold swastika is unchanged in all the years that it has been hidden in the lockbox.

But what of my memories, decades old and unavoidably inaccurate? No matter my devotion to preserving them, I have no lockbox. Instead, a mind. Not a brain, but whatever it is that animates my brain: a highly permeable assemblage of loves and fears and plans, strengths and frailties, desire and dread and the intent—dimly conscious at best—to manage all these in service of that slippery entity, *me*. Myself, as distinct from the rest of humanity. I try honorably to remember things as they really were, but the context in which I revisit a scene from my past—walking through a park, listening as my daughter practices piano, alone or in company—whatever my preoccupation, it necessarily contaminates the original. If biology, chemistry, and psychiatry can agree on anything, it is that memories are not received but created. What's more, they're subject to automatic, unavoidable revision. Under such circumstances, honor is useless.

Just last evening, my husband alluded to a mishap he believed he had witnessed. In 1994, our daughter, then four, and our son, two, stepped into an elevator while I was folding his stroller. I looked up, the doors closed, my children ascended without me. As we were in a big apartment building, with a whole bank of elevators, an hour of panic and tears elapsed before a woman who found them in the laundry room reunited the three of us in the lobby.

"You weren't there," I said, disagreeing with my husband.

"Yes, I was."

"No, if you'd been with us, if there had been two parents in that situation, it never would have happened."

"But I was sure I was there." He looked at me, confused.

"It's just that we've spoken of what happened enough times that you think you were with us, but you weren't." He nodded slowly, not quite convinced. "We could call Lori," I said. "She'll remember that it was just me and the kids." (Lori was the friend whom I'd taken our children to visit, and who enlisted her doorman and neighbors to help find and return them.)

My husband shrugged and went back to what he'd been reading. "That's okay," he said, choosing to believe me because I had the means to correct his misperception.

But what of my memories? There is nothing that unfolded in the house of my childhood that anyone can confirm, or deny. Countless transactions, most without consequence, but some fraught with significance—primal, formative, determinate—lack any witness other than myself. In the abstract, my being free of siblings, of parents, of anyone who might object to my dissembling, or even take note of an untruth, might provide me a tempting invitation to reinvent history. But only in the abstract, only in theory. When I test the idea, contemplating how completely possible it is to rewrite my early years, it frightens me. What I feel isn't freedom but a free fall, and what could check the speed of my descent? Humans agree that what we call "reality" depends on its being observed by at least one person. When a tree falls in my forest of memories and no one else hears it, has it happened? Is there a sound of one hand clapping? To be less philosophical, imagine yourself at a cocktail party, moving from one clot of guests to the next, one conversation to another. Are not these inadvertent opportunities for you to eavesdrop on your self as it slides from one context into another, shedding some pretenses, picking up others, revealing what, minutes before, it had hidden, sufficiently disturbing? If identity is fluid under these pedestrian circumstances, how reliable is the self whose past exists only inside her own head? How, without parents or siblings, can I really know what or who I was?

Among my memories, that part of my history represented by nothing more material than traces of neurochemicals in my cerebral cortex, Christmas morning 1966 has achieved the status of the gold swastika. It is the most puzzling and disturbing of all I possess. I woke up early, so early that it was still dark outside. But winter mornings were dark, and I was always up before my grandparents or my mother. I got out of bed; I didn't check the time. Either I couldn't yet read a clock or I was too intent on the stocking that hung from one of my bed's tall posts. My grandparents' house included a hearth that was greeting-card perfect for hanging a Christmas stocking; the mantel was carved from a massive oak beam and outfitted with hooks from which dangled pokers and pincers and bellows, even a bed warmer and a chestnut roaster, but I was not encouraged to leave my empty stocking in their company. I wonder if this wasn't because a single stocking looked too forlorn there by itself, too *only*.

I stood on the end of my bed to lift the bulging thing from over the post's finial, unobstructed by the bed's canopy, which had been removed because it gathered dust and made me wheeze. How satisfying was the stocking's weight and the way tissue paper wrappings crinkled from within it. This stocking was one I had inherited from my mother and it had her name, Carole, embroidered across its top. Below was an appliquéd tree of green wool felt, decorated with pea-size buttons made of colored glass and candles fashioned from minuscule strips of white patent leather, each about the size of half a toothpick, an orange bead for a flame. As if it were still hers, I carried the stocking to my mother's room to discover its contents with her. With regard to the issue of Santa Claus's identity, I teetered on a cusp between what I wished and what I feared. That it might have been my mother who assembled so perfect an array of tiny gifts, that she could have known me so well—enough to penetrate my desires and satisfy them—was a more seductive and cherished idea than that of a jolly old man who squeezed down chimneys. In service to the latter conceit, my grandfather effected the standard transformations, reducing the cookies and cocoa left on the mantel to crumbs and dregs, leaving a thank-you note written in an unfamiliar hand. And he performed a supplementary trick, dipping his shoes into the cold ashes and leaving a trail of footprints from there to my bedroom and back, a trail so convincing that I was afraid it was true, what I'd been told. Santa Claus, corpulent and sweating, had been far more perverse than I could have expected from my department-store visit to his red velour lap, criminal enough to break into our home and creep about while we slept.

As I wanted the stocking to be my mother's work, I intended to watch her as I unpacked it, in order to gauge her investment in my pleasure. I remember—I can see—my mother's bed as I entered her room. Moonlight was sufficient to reveal that it had not been slept in. I stood for some minutes holding the stocking and trying to imagine a benign reason for her absence. Was there such one?

Had I a brother or a sister, I would have gone at once to his or her room that we might confer over this unexpected—alarming—turn of events. But I was alone, and so I walked by myself through the hall to the shadowy living room, anxious speculations about my mother's whereabouts rendering me immune to the sinister power of a portrait whose subject, I'd convinced myself, climbed out of her frame to do mischief unobserved. Having determined that my mother was nowhere in the house, I went to my grandmother's bedside and touched her shoulder. A light sleeper, she woke instantly and sat forward rather than up from her pillows, piled high to keep her that much more upright and offset the breathlessness caused by her rheumatic heart.

"What?" she said. "What is it?" When I told her, she swung her feet over the side of the bed and stamped one in anger. "If that doesn't—" she began, but she didn't finish. Instead, she snapped on the light and woke my grandfather. "Gone!" she announced to his startled countenance. "How do you like that! She's gone! Sneaked off in the middle of the night!"

Immediately I understood that alerting my grandmother to my mother's disappearance had been the exactly wrong response. My mother wasn't lost—she'd escaped. And I had betrayed her; I, who was always searching to discover a means of ingratiating myself, of proving my worth to my remote and distracted young mother, of insinuating myself between her and the lovely reflection in her mirror, between her and the novel in her lap, between her and the telephone receiver in her hand. Meaning well, I had done something awful and irrevocable.

The fight my mother had with my grandmother later that morning, when she accused my mother of being a—what word would she have used? Not "slut." Certainly not "whore." Well, whatever my grandmother did or didn't say, their fight was what my mother would end up calling "the last last straw, the absolute, final end." "Tart"? Maybe, except "tart" wasn't a word my grandmother used in anger. She thought "tart" was funny. Ditto "trollop." "Cheap," I guess. She might have called my mother "cheap" for sneaking out to spend the night with a boyfriend. "Cheap," like other comparatively mild slurs, was a word my grandmother could pronounce as a dire insult. But just as possibly, she might have used no words, she might have just screamed: That was a standard, and unanswerable, strategy. My grandmother's inarticulate, animal howls, which seemed to presage madness or violence, or both, often won her an argument, either because of their inherent power to terrorize or because they testified to her ruthlessness, her stop-at-nothing determination to win. A month or two later, my mother moved out, for good. Unwittingly, I had been the catalyst for my own abandonment.

THE PAINTER RENÉ MAGRITTE remembered the suicide of his mother, Regina, as happening in this way. In 1912, Magritte, the youngest in the family, was fourteen. He shared a bedroom with his mother, and one night awoke to find her gone. He roused the rest of the household, and they searched but could find her nowhere inside. But beyond the front door, traces of her steps led to a nearby bridge over the river Sambre, in whose waters René and his brothers saw their mother's lifeless body. Louis Scutenaire, the artist's lifelong friend, has related Magritte's version of the story, in which the boy René watched as his mother's corpse was pulled from the water, her face covered by her nightdress, her body naked, luminously white in the moonlight.

Asked what they remembered of the death of Mme. Magritte, the artist's childhood friends recalled that though they themselves had all cried in fear and grief, René betrayed no emotion in the weeks following his mother's suicide and from that point forward never spoke of her. As a famous painter, Magritte gave many interviews; in all of these he mentioned his mother's death no more than two times. Asked (rather idiotically) if the event had "marked" him, he said only that it had been a "shock." His 1954 outline for an autobiography included a single, abbreviated reference, in the third rather than the first person: "In 1912, his mother, Regina, does not want to live anymore. She throws herself in Sambre."

The thing is, though Magritte did wake to discover that his mother's bed was empty, he never saw her body recovered from the river. As a number of onlookers, including his older brothers, testified, the boy wasn't there on the banks.

Psychology, a science Magritte dismissed as false, an attempt to explain what cannot be explained, to render irreducible mystery to pedestrian cause and effect, calls such memories as his own of his mother's body in the river "screen memories," which typically date back to childhood and which a child creates to protect himself from a truth he finds even more traumatic than what he invents to hide it. But what could be worse than the scene Magritte believed he witnessed? The face of his dead mother unveiled? Her body, for which he must have harbored—as all children do—a desire to possess, covered by a winding sheet and taken from him forever? A desire enflamed at the time of her death, when, caught up in the turmoil of adolescence, he still shared her bedroom, saw her in a nightdress that revealed perhaps a little more than it ought?

"It may indeed be questioned whether we have any memories at all from our childhood," Freud writes in his 1899 paper on the topic. "Memories relating to childhood may be all that we possess."

It is only as I consider my early years with the express purpose of divining how I feel, or felt, about having been an only child that I understand—suddenly and with no little anxiety—why this story of Magritte and his mother's suicide has compelled and disturbed me for so many years. Ever since I learned of it (accidentally, while pursuing the larger topic of memory and how reliably true it might or might not be) I've revisited the scene over and over, trying to picture the artist as he might have pictured himself, seeing a boy, a boy the same age as my son is now—how clearly, then, can I imagine his form, the slope of his shoulders, the balled fists at his sides—as he stands on the river's bank in the moonlit night. Of course, the body frightens the boy in its faceless nakedness, flesh I see as if rendered by the surrealist himself, gray and shadowed, like the shuttered house in his 1954 painting *Empire of Light*, a simple nighttime landscape made sinister by its having an impossible daylit sky.

Magritte and I knew only the same few facts: One night we awoke; we found our mother's bed empty; we alerted our families; a tragedy ensued. That the artist's story, far more dire than my own, included a set of ghostly footprints leading to a terrible truth would appeal, naturally, to a child who followed the ashy tracks of a Christmas intruder who threatened to steal an idea she valued above material possessions: that, contrary to appearances, her mother had been paying her careful attention all along. But if

Magritte unconsciously fabricated a narrative to explain his terror—
a story his brothers and friends denied—might the Christmas memory in question, over which I've puzzled for forty years—holding
it dear as one guards the instrument of a dangerous wound (the
way, for example, a soldier might preserve a piece of shrapnel dug
out of his chest)—might that morning never have happened? Or
might it have happened very differently from the way I believe
it did?

The pieces of the story are, all of them, emblematic of my early
unhappiness. My mother's bed that she hadn't slept in was the bed
I visited each day after she moved out, standing before the lie it
spoke, its sheets changed weekly as if to suggest that her return
was imminent. The Christmas stocking, whose contents I fetishized
and displayed each year, never playing with the toys but arranging
them in a tableau on my dresser, was a perfect symbol for a mother
who removed herself from the realm of the everyday to become a
kind of holiday apparition. The night itself, when Christmas Eve
becomes Christmas Day and a child's worthiness—her naughti-
ness or niceness—is judged and found either sufficient or wanting, well represents my fascination with the idea of my goodness
and what it might afford me—if not the return of my mother, then
some other reward, someone else's admiration. The bedpost with
its missing canopy evokes asthma, an ever-present threat of suffocation (and the grandmother, too, propped up on her pillows to
avoid feeling smothered). And, finally, isn't the most troubling aspect of the memory, that it was my actions that caused my mother
to leave me, too neatly textbook to be true? Don't all children hold
themselves responsible for their abandonment?

Do I remember this night so vividly, with a heightened, almost hallucinatory attention to detail, because it represents my childhood so perfectly, or have I unconsciously collected and/or fabricated symbols of my past to assemble them into a story in order that I might contain them within the mnemonic device of a narrative so as not to lose these critical aspects of myself? Just as the initial letters of the words of the sentence "Every Good Boy Does Fine" might help a young musician retrieve the notes of the treble clef staff, this memory—true or false—provides me a place to safeguard pieces of my early childhood.

Within the embrace of psychotherapy, in whose arms I've spent an hour each week for fifteen years, "the feelings are the facts." Which is all very well, assuming the availability of reality checks. Of, say, a brother or sister who might call me on the claim of straight A's: "There must have been a frigging B in there somewhere," he'd say. "PE," I'd answer, "and that doesn't count." But maybe it would count to my brother, the one I don't have. He might be an athlete, a perfect uncle for my son, who dreams of becoming a star baseball player. Or what about my sister, who might say, in her intimate knowledge of my flaws, "Piss off. You're always hiding inside your head, behind your good grades." But I wouldn't waste their voices on my grades—for topics like that I have my boxes in the basement.

I didn't mind being an only child when I was a child. I understood the bargain it implied, that if I'd had siblings I would have lost my monopoly over my grandparents' affection, halve or even more drastically reduce my mother's infrequent attention. Like most children, I knew the stresses of the family in which I'd landed: a pair of guardians who were, respectively, seventy-one and sixty-two at my birth, old if not frail; a child-mother who never

grew up; endless conflicts arising from our dwindling financial resources. Another child in the family would have applied that
much more pressure to what was already as frayed as the carpets
and drapes, the sprung sofa upholstered in an impractical pink
chintz. Another child would have endangered me.

But, as an adult, having long ago reached the age at which I'd
expected to have left my only childhood far behind, I mind it very
much. I want a witness—or better, two, three—to what I remember,
a person or persons to whom I could turn and ask, "Remember
that Christmas, the one when Mom . . ."

A Pair of Onlies

ALYSIA ABBOTT

Serene stands the little captain, he's not hurried. His
voice is neither high nor low. His eyes give more light to
us than our battle lanterns. —*Walt Whitman*

*I*N 1976, DAD *was thirty-two and a single father. He had a dark
brown handlebar mustache and wore plaid button-up shirts over
white T-shirts, sleeves rolled up to his elbows. He was trying to find
work, any work, to supplement the Social Security check that arrived by
mail each week after my mom's fatal car crash three years earlier. And
whenever he could, he'd go out, searching for love in the bars of the Castro
and the Haight. "I'm a poet," he used to tell the strange young men.
And in San Francisco in 1976, this still meant something. He was
struggling to find his voice, visiting used-book stores, trying to find his
community. He wrote on spiral notebooks in cafés or at home when I
wasn't jumping all over his lap, craving some kind of attention, some
kind of something that he didn't quite know how to satisfy.*

*At four years old, soon to be five, I wanted only simple things: car-
toons and French toast, a dog or a cat, not doves or guppies, which we
had. But more than a dog to wrestle or a cat to pet, I wanted my dad. I
wanted him to myself to cling to, to sleep with, to feed me, and to eat*

with. I wanted to crawl back into wherever I'd crawled out of, away from the unpredictable world around us.

Often, Dad obliged me. We'd play hide-and-seek in the park. At home, he'd make me spaghetti. We'd "whestle awound the woom," tussling until I was red-faced and out of breath. Then we'd watch TV or he'd read me stories. But there were also nights when he went to bars, or to places I didn't know about, and left me with other people. These not-my-dad people tried to be nice to me; they fed me dinner and played with me a little but were not him. No cigarette-scented him with loving hands holding me, no warm lap that quaked whenever he laughed his enormous up-and-down laugh. No skinny chest I listened to as it vibrated in animated conversation.

Other nights, I'd accompany him to potluck dinner parties or to bookstore poetry readings where the adults crowded the room, a forest of legs for me to push through to find my dad against some wall deep in conversation. When I found him, I'd crawl into his lap or lie on the floor next to where he stood, waiting for time to pass. On the drive home from these parties, I'd inevitably fall asleep in our Volkswagen Bug. Even if I woke up, I'd pretend to be sleeping so that he would carry me from the parked car, up the three flights of stairs to our apartment, and into my bed.

IN 1992, I CLUNG to any means to leave the house. At twenty-one, I longed to feel a part of the tattooed, grunge-tinged scene that permeated the cafés and bars in San Francisco's lower Haight. Wearing big hoop earrings, men's white V-necked T-shirts with jeans and my father's black suit vest, I flirted with boys and sometimes even forgot why I was in San Francisco and not in New York. I'd graduated a semester early from NYU. As my father's only daughter, I made a promise to leave school early and to care for him, now that he was sick. I made a promise to move back home, a promise that I had mixed feelings about making.

When I first returned to our Haight-Ashbury apartment, I rocked wildly in my fury, my weary waste. I was too accessible then, too present in his homebound world. Waiting for responses to job applications, I'd linger next to my father's bed, watching him count out pills. I'd accompany him to all of his doctor's appointments. And with few friends or activities to distract me I easily fell into deep pits of despair and lethargy. Then I got busy. I took weekly GRE classes to improve my chances of getting into graduate schools to which I'd never apply. And eventually I found a nine-to-five job selling videotape of the news to Fortune 500 companies, and an internship at a local college radio station. Nights, I met up with Scott, who worked in a popular lower-Haight café and who was the bass player in an up-and-coming local band, Heavy Into Jeff. Scott helped remind me that at my age, I was meant to be enjoying carefree sex, not suffering the demands and needs of a dying father. But even after a passionate session with him, I still couldn't forget. I'd burst into tears holding tightly to his thick arms while he sat rocking me, saying nothing.

Back at home I was always, again, my father's daughter, his only child. I was a nurse, cleaning up next to the toilet where he'd missed. A maid, picking up the dirty glasses and stiff, crumpled tissues that gathered around his bed, and buying gallon after gallon of juice to replenish the fluids lost during his night sweats.

Some weekends Dad would accompany me to Café Flore in the Castro, but others he'd stay in bed violently coughing, distracting me from my GRE studies or painfully reinserting his illness into my healthy world. I even once yelled out, *"Shut up!"* from my desk. I believed he hadn't heard me until he brought up the incident later, shaming me. "I cough so much I think I'm going to throw up. I can't help it."

To comfort him, I'd run the vacuum cleaner, not to clean the house but because he liked the sound. He told me it reminded him of being a little boy at home in Lincoln, Nebraska, with his mother. As he huddled beneath the bedcovers, the vacuum cleaner would hum loudly, upright and immobile next to his bed, while I, sitting on the sofa beside him, reveled in self-pity, feeling heavy and doomed.

One night when I was four, my dad wanted to bring me out with him to a reading. I told him I wanted to stay home. No sitter was available, but he let me stay in anyway. Alone.

"Don't answer the door," he said. "Just stay here and play with your little people."

I put on a brave face. I was a big girl. And after he left me I decided to do what he might have done, like a big girl does: I washed my hair.

In the bathroom by the porcelain tub I found a clear bottle filled with yellow shampoo. I emptied this bottle into my hand, then massaged the globs into my hair, like Dad did each week. I can't remember if I wet my hair, but I do remember lathering it into a foam of bubbles and sticky heft. My head was too heavy for my body as I tried to stick it under the bathtub faucet; I couldn't get my head under the water. My hair seemed to drip, a mass of mess served up on my shoulders, unraveling and falling all over me. The soap dripped down into my face and made my eyes sting and tear. And I was scared because I didn't know what to do. I cried, but no one answered. The water kept running, the hair kept dripping, my eyes kept stinging, but still no one answered. I shut off the water and tried to walk my heavy mass of head into the living room where I could play with my little people and try to make the wet hair go away.

Sometime later, the door unlocked with a pop and there was my father. I was thrilled to see him, to know that he had come back and that I was no longer alone. But his face quickly turned angry as he saw me playing on the living-room floor with my wet hair, surrounded by a trail of suds and pools of water.

"Why did you do this?" he demanded. His face was red. His green eyes bulged.

In the bathroom he picked up the empty bottle. He wasn't happy. He had his sleeves rolled up past his elbows so he wouldn't get them wet, and he sat me in the tub. He perched on the tub's edge and began to rinse my head under the bathtub faucet. It hurt. All the tangles and knots pulled at my head. I started to cry because I couldn't tell him what he wanted to hear. I could read his anger, but I didn't understand where it came from. What could I have done wrong? Hadn't he come home to save me from the dripping water and stinging suds that I couldn't contain?

FIFTEEN YEARS LATER, I leave *him* alone. I jump on my mountain bike, soar down Haight, past the hills of Divisadero, down to Market and South of Market to my job at Video Monitoring Service. When I return that evening, his mere presence on the foldout futon, in the same position in front of the television where I'd left him eight hours earlier, is oppressive to me. After months of living at home, I've long since exchanged my fantasies of the fearlessness of the fatally ill—Stealing cars! Jumping out of planes! Nothing left to lose and the world theirs for the taking!—for the tiresome reality of nurse visits and pill vials and Open Hand meals delivered night after night by another kind-faced stranger.

"How was your day?" he asks me.

"My day was fine," I grumble, resting my bike against the dining-room table. Unbuckling my helmet, I ask, "How was yours?"

"Well." He chuckles sheepishly, "I was heating up the Open Hand meal for lunch, then I fell asleep and it burned."

"So you didn't eat?"

"No."

Hearing my father's pitiful no, I feel myself propelled from his room, eager to jump back onto my bike and head to Scott's place.

HE SHOULD NEVER have left me alone when I was only four. But then, had I not left him alone now, maybe he wouldn't have burned his Open Hand meal and he would have eaten. Maybe he wouldn't have tried to change the dining-room light on his own. He wouldn't have dropped the glass lamp shade and he wouldn't have cut his finger.

I wrestled with my conscience then, and I wrestle with it still. Wouldn't the *good* daughter have found a way to stay home? Shouldn't this have been the time when we became even closer, exchanging dark secrets and final wishes? But staying at home was never a consideration for me. I'd left real friends and real work opportunities when I left New York City. My life now was just beginning. Why should it come to a standstill simply because his was coming to an end? And with the ups and downs of my father's sickness, even this end was maddeningly vague and unplannable.

I needed a vibrant self, separate from *daughter* and *caretaker*.

Just as now I imagine my father needed to be someone other than Dad when he was caring for me.

As a girl I used to fantasize about the other life I might have known had my mother not gone out that night in 1973, had her car not been rear-ended, sending her flying through the window and into the street. She and my dad would have continued what I imagined was their storybook love affair. Without the burden of grief, my dad would never have turned gay. And surely they would have had more kids. In this other world, we'd live not in a one-bedroom city apartment but in a large suburban house with a car and a garage and a yard. I'd be the big sister, the leader of a rowdy clan who stayed close together, putting on plays, and warding off neighborhood bullies. But as much as I longed for the normalness and comfort of a big family, I also loved being my father's daughter, his only child.

The meals my father prepared for the two of us seemed uniquely suited to our single-parent, single-child family. He'd buy a single chicken leg for us to share, bake it until the skin was crispy golden yellow and the juice and butter pooled together on the tinfoil lining our pan, then he'd cut the leg in two, keeping the thigh for himself and giving the perfect-size drumstick to me.

For dessert, we'd split a package of Hostess CupCakes, which were sold in twos. I developed elaborate methods of eating mine to prolong the experience, holding the cupcake upside down in my cupped palm, eating the spongy cake first, then the white center, finishing with the chocolate frosting and, finally, the hardened white-sugar squiggle.

Sweets were an indulgence we shared. Just as I would pool pennies to buy myself candy after school, Dad would eat bags of Hershey's Kisses each time he tried to quit smoking. Having just enough cupcakes for *ourselves and no more for anyone else only heightened the romance of our situation. We were a pair of onlies. We were singles together, and I wouldn't have had it any other way.*

"I DON'T THINK I can do this much longer," I announced one evening, balanced on the edge of his futon bed.

And he smiled. The light from his eyes shone at me serenely, even though his vessel was failing, while mine was still young and sturdy.

"Of course you can; you can do anything you set your mind to."

Peacefully, he lay in bed. The television was blaring, yet only I seemed to hear the penetrating noise. It washed over him like a harmless wave. He was the rock then. And I was free-floating and wild.

Rocking back and forth in my seat, I continued with my plan. "I need a limit. A year. I moved in here Christmas and after next Christmas I want to move out, maybe go back to New York.

"I don't think I can do this," I repeated. "I'm not ready for this." Then he answered me, his words a slap.

"I wasn't ready to care for you when your mother died. But I did."

WHEN I WAS A GIRL my father never questioned me when I wanted to stay home from school sick. He never felt my forehead or stared suspiciously into my eyes, trying to catch my lie. He'd answer, "Fine," when I said I wasn't feeling well, and shoo me back to my bedroom and to bed, a wooden loft he had built for my ninth birthday. Back between my sheets I could hear my father in the kitchen mixing the cherry Jell-O, pausing between beats to take a drag off his Carlton

regulars. I could hear him slicing the bananas that would float in the
Jell-O mold's shallow waters. This was step one in our sick-day ritual.
While the Jell-O was cooling in the fridge, he'd buy comic books—Mad
magazines and Betty & Veronica—*for me to read in bed. And for*
lunch he'd serve me Campbell's Chunky Chicken Noodle soup, a fa-
vorite of ours.

ON A WEDNESDAY morning, my father is lying on the futon
mattress while I busy myself at the dining-room table, stacking
*San Francisco Chronicle*s, sorting mail. I've taken the day off from
work so that I can move him into the hospice. A friend will pick us
up in her car at noon. Through the heavy curtain separating my father's room from the dining room, I can hear him clear his throat.

"I don't see how we can possibly be ready by noon." Dad is in
one of his moods. But I'm in one of mine, too.

"Noon?! That's four hours from now," I respond. "We've plenty
of time."

"I sometimes don't get up until afternoon. It seems rushed to
me. I get exhausted just walking to the bathroom."

"I'll do the packing. You won't have to worry about anything.
Just sit there. I'm here for you. Do you understand that? That's
why I was born," I say.

"They call it 'attendant care' when all they do is intrude on my
life. They poke and prod and say, '*Now here have this medicine . . .*
have that.'"

"Is that the way they are at the hospice?"

"That's the way they are at the hospital," he says.

"You're going to the hospice, not the hospital. You don't know what they are going to be like. Do you even know where you are going, Dad?"

No answer.

THREE HOURS LATER:

"Do you want an egg-salad sandwich before we drive to the hospice?"

"Half of one," he says.

"There's half a chicken sandwich in the fridge, isn't there?"

"It's a chicken sandwich and I don't want a chicken sandwich."

"It's pretty hard to make only half a sandwich. Are you sure you don't want a whole sandwich and save the other half for later if you can't finish it?"

"All I want is half of a sandwich. I already said that. Do I have to draw a picture?"

After boiling the egg, I crack off the shell and smash it in a bowl with a spoonful of mayonnaise and a dollop of Dijon mustard. I spread this mixture in between two slices of wheat bread, cut the sandwich in half, and lay one half on a plate and the other half in the fridge next to the half-eaten chicken sandwich.

"Do you even appreciate that I took the day off?" I ask him.

"I'm sorry. I guess I'm kind of grumpy today." I can understand why my father fought with me that day. People didn't move into the hospice to live but to die.

I RAISED HIM through his sickness much like he had raised me through his health. But though he was little, wee in his shrunken frame, he was still the captain. Silently, cleverly in control. He knew well the power of the powerless, the steel of the rubber spine. He could refuse to eat my meals. And though the hospice provided TVs for all of their residents, he refused to leave home without his own. "I'll raise such a fuss they won't take me!" he exclaimed. I pulled a muscle carrying it up the stairs to his room.

AFTER MY FATHER died, I again reveled in my onliness. Perhaps my father's family, all living in the Midwest, would have come out in those final months of his life had I urged them. Perhaps, too, my father's friends could have helped me sort the twenty-year accumulation of things I had to slowly sift through in the months following his death. But if anyone had been available, if anyone had entered the delicate two-step of our final year together, then my "only" status would have been threatened. I'd have had to share the noble light of caregiving. And if I was going to have to suffer through my dad's death, damned if I was going to share that noble light with anyone.

It didn't occur to me until after my dad died that the lack of a long-term boyfriend in his life, someone who would have helped me cope with his death, was due, at least in part, to my overarching presence in our apartment. I had scowled, I was rude, I neglected to deliver phone messages. Except for a close attachment to my father's first two boyfriends, the men who passed through our life were all useless to me. They could never replace my mother. And neither could they give birth to the brothers and sisters who could round out our little clan. All they could do was take my father from me, divide his precious love in two.

There were two separate memorial services for my father: one organized by his family in Lincoln, Nebraska, and one in San Francisco, attended by my father's adopted family, his community

of poets, critics, lovers, intellectuals, and freaks. With this second
audience, I held a singular position. As the only child, the only attending relation, I had pride of place. *I* chose the large photo to
display at the Buddhist ceremony in the basement of the Hartford
Street Zen Center—a commanding black-and-white portrait of my
father that had hung in our apartment. *I* chose an excerpt from
one of his essays, which I photocopied and distributed at the
service. *I* picked the poem to be read at the service's close. And
alone I read it.

The service is held on December 11, 1992. As the sole heir to
my father's meager estate, I drape myself in his heavy leather mo-
torcycle jacket. It hangs on my shoulders, my frame now shrunken
from the stress of those final months.

The resident monk, Phil Whalen, tall and bald and large in a
long blue robe, performs the ceremony, chanting sutras and lighting incense. Smoke snakes through the air. The ceilings are low.
The room seems small. And in my father's leather jacket, I'm
warm. At first, I stand along with everyone in the cramped basement space, where my father and the other Maitri members
would sit zazen every week. Perspiration trickles down my neck
and back. It could be nerves. After Phil's reading, I take the stage.

I look into the mass of bodies all standing at attention, awaiting
my delivery. I hold my father's book *Stretching the Agape Bra* in my
hands. On the cover we're posed together alone: an unsmiling
Gothic father and his unsmiling ten-year-old daughter. He wears a
pinstripe suit and two-tone shoes, and holds a long-stemmed
white flower. I stand behind him in a high-necked white dress,
with one arm to my side and one behind my back. He'd taken me
out of my fifth-grade class so that I could pose with him that day in

Golden Gate Park. Folding the pages back I turn to the book's last poem, "Elegy."

In the poem, my father imagines what it's like to die. He imagines first losing his sense of sight, then sound, touch, taste, and, finally, smell. He sees his spirit floating up after being burned at the stake. He liked to imagine himself in ancient history. Taking my father's words in my mouth, I mimic the rhythms I'd learned accompanying him to scores of readings, often the only child in the room. Commanding this audience to listen to me, I feel powerful. My voice never wavers, even when reading the lines he wrote about me:

Babar's mother was killed by a mean hunter and that makes Alysia sad even now.

My father stares out from behind me in his black-and-white incarnation. In the photo, he is handsome, his face still almost plump in 1989. He wears his black button-down shirt and his Jesus bolo tie. He's not smiling, but staring serenely at the camera's lens with wet, light eyes, watching in a sort of knowing, affectionate way.

I continue reading, sensing him there, saying to me, *You, yes you. Who else could read this but you?*

You're It

Betty Rollin

You're it. That's the bottom line. If you're the son, you must also be the daughter. If you're the daughter, you must be the son, too. You might also be the dog, if your parents are missing one of those. You're the hope, the dreams; and you're the one and the only one to blame if it doesn't turn out all right. Which is to say, if *you* don't turn out all right—according, of course, to your parents' definition of "all right." It's not that people with siblings don't experience the same sort of pressure. The difference is that all the pressure, all the focus, is on little old you. If your parents want, say, a brilliant child, and you're not brilliant, no problem if you've got a sibling. And even if the sibling is no more brilliant than you, you can be dumb together.

I, myself, the only child of upwardly striving Jews, was not expected to be brilliant. I was a girl, after all, born in 1936. But I was expected to be smart, also good, pretty (oh, those curls), sweet, affectionate, musical (oh, those Sunday afternoon piano lessons), graceful, and well-spoken (oh, those Saturday ballet, art, and elocution lessons). And that was only childhood.

Did I mind? Of course not. Kids don't mind stuff until they get older and then they mind mainly in retrospect. I did notice that the kids across the street in Yonkers, mostly Irish working class, were not under the gun the way I was, at least not in the same way. Their parents didn't care if they said Toosday instead of Tyoosdy, which is how I learned to say it in elocution class. Their little paintings, if indeed they did little paintings, were taped onto the refrigerator, not framed and hammered into the wall.

I noticed something else about the Irish kids across the street. When it was not quite bedtime and the lights were still on in their bedrooms—two, shared by five kids—they were all having a grand old time, or so it seemed to me. I had my own room and the only other person in it, briefly, was my mother to say good night and linger for a moment while I said my prayers. The Irish kids thought I was lucky to have my own room. Some of them, I know, also felt I was lucky to have my mother, who was always having all the neighborhood kids over for treats and games. I see now what she was doing. She was importing siblings. Sweet of her, really. It was probably then I learned that whereas for most people friends are nice to have, for me—and other onlies—friends are necessary.

When I was about fifteen, I found out my birthday was not a national holiday. My mother truly went crazy on my birthday. There were always at least four parties: one for her family, one for my father's family, one for her friends, one for my friends. I got piles of presents, of course. But then my parents were always giving me things, birthday or not. My protests went unheeded. "I don't need another doll [or pair of mittens, or whatever]," I'd wail. My mother paid no attention. All of this had the following lifelong effect on me: I don't require presents. (Luckily, I married someone who feels the same way. If my husband bought me a piece of jewelry for, say, Valentine's Day, I would be alarmed. Then, whatever it was, I'd return it.)

My father did not obsess over me the way my mother did. But he went along. And since my mother worked—as a schoolteacher, and later as my father's sort-of office manager—they hired a German housekeeper I called Nana, who also went along. I loved Nana, not only because she let me eat bologna sandwiches, but because I could whine to her when my mother got to be too much. Nana couldn't criticize my mother, of course, but I knew she was on my side, which was enough. Nevertheless, there she was: yet another adult focused on me.

It seems to me I spent most of my childhood longing to be neglected.

As I grew older, my mother got more intense about the shaping of me, her only creation. She decided I had to go to private school. She did research and through something highfalutin called the Child Study Association learned that the two best schools—in their opinion—were a Quaker school in Brooklyn and the Fieldston School in Riverdale. My father rarely put his foot down, but he came close to it when the Quaker idea came up. My father came to the United States from Russia when he was twenty and lived through some pretty intense anti-Semitism, which led to a strong Jewish identity; the notion of a Christian school pained him. Fortunately—for him, anyway—my mother thought Brooklyn was too distant from Yonkers, so Fieldston it was.

Just as I loved many of the things my mother pushed on me—

ballet, painting, elocution—I loved Fieldston. I was a bit cowed by the sophistication of my classmates, who lived in Manhattan and rode the subway and had dates in Schrafft's—a now-extinct tearoomy sort of place—but I soon adjusted and felt lucky to be there.

The feeling of being lucky was an outgrowth of a new realization that we weren't rich, as I had always thought we were. I knew this because at Fieldston, the kids were truly rich. The first clue was the cashmere sweater sets and the second was the number— more than two—of bathrooms they all had in their apartments. With that realization came the accompanying thought that if I had a sibling, which I fantasized about occasionally, I would not only get less stuff, but I might not even get Fieldston or, later, summer camp, which I found thrilling because of my mother's absence. (Of course, she sent me weekly packages that included prunes.) The siblings in my fantasies were brothers, one older brother, actually, who would protect me from my mother. I didn't covet sisters until many years later when I saw how nice it could be to have a family member who doubled as a friend. Not having one of those, I've always tried to make my friends into family. This, I think, is what onlies often do, but it doesn't altogether work. Water is thinner than blood, and friends are not stuck with you in perpetuity the way siblings are. In addition, friends usually have siblings—or children, not to mention parents and/or husbands. All of those people understandably come first.

When I was a small child, as I recall, my mother's perpetual gaze was entirely adoring. I was the most beautiful, the most wonderful, the smartest, the best. That changed.

In adolescence, as I began to pull away, I began to hear, "Why

228 • YOU'RE IT

don't you comb your hair? . . . You're cold. How could you be so
cold when you have such a warm, loving family? . . . You think
you're smart, but you're only book-smart." And so on. Nana was
still around, but she couldn't protect me from all of that.

I began to hate my mother. And, of course, I was alone in my
hatred.

By now it must be obvious: To be an only child and to be the
only child of my particular mother are not the same. I stopped hat-
ing my mother when I stopped fearing her. It took a long time.
Getting older helped. Psychoanalysis helped. Getting married
helped. (She loved both of my husbands, even the not-so-hot one.)
Cancer helped. When I got breast cancer, nothing frightened me
except it. Also, my mother came through big-time. She was cheery
(but not too cheery) and strong, and all criticism of me was put on
hold. We reverted to my childhood, when I was perfect. No siblings needed now.

It kind of stayed that way. She never stopped giving me what
she called "advice," but somehow I found that more funny than
annoying. Maybe because we both knew that she had no power of
enforcement, even through guilt. Besides, occasionally her advice
was right. Gradually, she moved into the category of best friend.
That is, she was the person I telephoned most, not from duty or
fear, but out of wanting to tell her things and ask her things.

Then she got sick, horribly sick. Ovarian cancer. She got to a
point where she wanted to die, and I loved her enough to help her.
(It's a long story—a book, in fact.) My husband was totally with
me during all of this and in effect became my sibling. But after it
was all over and I officially entered orphanhood, he went back to
being just my husband. (My father had died in 1975—the same

year I had breast cancer.) With no children or siblings, I began to long for both, especially a sister. I wanted a sister to share my grief over losing "our" mother. I wanted a sister to talk with me about "our" childhood. I wanted a sister to explain things to me I never understood, like why my mother never had more children. Somehow, I never found out, only that it took seven years for her to have me, and after that her body couldn't seem to do it again.

What does only childhood do to a person? I'm certainly self-centered; on the other hand, I think I'm less needy of attention than those who experienced the kind of childhood neglect I longed for. I have close friendships, but sometimes I'm too demanding. I give a lot to my friends, but I want a lot back. I want love from them and often I get only like.

I read a lot, a habit I developed in childhood when there was no one to play with.

My marriage has worked. Perhaps it wouldn't have worked so well if we had had children and I had competition. Just a guess. It's all just a guess. Life as an only child shapes you, but so do a trillion other things, some of which have to do with parents, others not. Like, in my case, getting cancer at a fairly young age.

Still, when an only child gets a disease like cancer, there's an added bit of . . . shall I call it tension? I remember my parents in the hospital room, one on each side of my bed, looking down at me; I felt obliged to them in a way I hadn't for a long time. They could and did absorb my being sick. But I knew I couldn't die.

NEW YEAR'S EVE 1997

TELLER

PARENTS ARE CAREGIVERS. Kids are cared for. That's the grammar of the family. A kid must never appear to be caring for his parents—lest he rob his parents of their very definition.

If you're an only child, and you love your parents, and your parents need you, well, what do you do? You help them while pretending not to help. You lie. And you think you fool them.

But your parents are the ultimate lie detector. They've watched you too closely and known you too long. So isn't it more likely your parents are pretending to be fooled—in order to care for their deceitful kid?

BY THE TIME my parents were in their eighties, I had studied deception and sleight of hand for more than forty years, and was touring almost year-round with my magic show, Penn & Teller. When I noticed my parents needing a bit more help, I started arranging my schedule to allow for travel through Philadelphia, where my parents lived, every month or so.

I'd present myself as a weary vagabond in need of a good dinner. My parents would make up the bed in my room with clean sheets, and would spend days peeling, pickling, and roasting in preparation for a homecoming feast.

Once they'd fed me and lodged me for a night, it was only natural for me to offer to "earn my keep." Sometimes I would rent a car—my parents would insist on paying for it—and take Mam (my mother, a tiny, roundish, white-haired engine of love and willpower) to a spectacular South Philadelphia supermarket, where she would fill two shopping carts with mountains of meat and enough canned goods to last till the next ice age.

Other times I'd make repairs to my parents' three-and-a-half-story Lincoln-era brick row house under the step-by-step instruction of Pad (my father, a bald wiseacre with failing sight and a penchant for the mot juste).

Sometimes I even persuaded my parents to go out for plain old fun: to the Red Lobster seafood restaurant (where they loved the shrimp and biscuits); to buy socks at Target; or to lounge on the banks of the beautiful Schuylkill River, where we'd all merrily heave bread to the ducks.

Eventually, I was booked into a long run in Las Vegas. That restricted my visits still further. I had to become more devious in my caregiving. Mam and Pad clearly needed frequent help. But they had worked all their lives, and would not consider hiring a "servant" to work for them. So I found an accomplice at Philadelphia's City Hall who contacted Mam and Pad and convinced them that their years as faithful Philadelphia taxpayers had entitled them to a city-funded "home health aide," a person who could come in and assist with cleaning and shopping.

As an experienced magician, I knew such a trick would require considerable "misdirection"—the conjuring term for the minor lie that gives the major lie credibility. So I arranged for my accomplice to come visit my parents and make them fill out tedious forms, just to make the process credibly humiliating. After a plausible bureaucratic delay, I then secretly engaged a local nursing service to help with shopping and cleaning as often as my parents would tolerate it.

I also adopted a "brother" in Philadelphia, a friend-of-a-friend named J. He was a young actor/director who, at the time, sustained himself as Thomas Jefferson in Philadelphia's historical district. J. had a mysterious way of showing up at my parents' house for a friendly visit whenever he was most needed. At Thanksgiving, if I couldn't be there, J. might find himself "burdened" with gourmet leftovers and ask my parents' help in "getting rid of them." One evening when my mother needed medical help, J. came straight from Independence Hall and whisked her off to the emergency room, where he sat in full Thomas Jefferson colonial costume for nine hours until Mam was seen by the doctors and returned home safe.

I phoned my parents daily from wherever I was. "Hello, this is The Kid," I'd say, and start off with some story about being on the road with my show, or at home in Las Vegas. In return, my parents would tell me about their day. Their stories always sounded spontaneous, but thinking back on them, I'm guessing my parents— especially Pad—spent a part of their day composing the anecdotes for my pleasure. For example:

Pad: "Would you like to know how to catch a fly in the house on a sunny day? First, open the back kitchen door. Leave the outside screen door closed, but make sure it is not locked. Close the blinds, then turn off all the lights inside the house. Then wait till the sun shines on the screen. Sooner or later the fly will go to the sunlight. Quietly close the door behind him. Now go out the side door and out to the door where the fly is trapped. Open the screen door and the fly will fly away to annoy other people. I think even the SPCA would approve."

This kind of fable, whether true or fabricated—Pad taught me to always choose humor over fact in storytelling—inspired me to start writing down the things my parents said in those phone calls and during my visits. Writing about your parents helps you in two regards: While they live, it helps you understand and appreciate them; when they're gone, it helps keep them alive in your heart. My parents were generous enough to live for a full eight years after I acquired the sense to begin that notebook.

All of this is by way of introducing a little excerpt from The Kid's diary, the notes I made on New Year's Eve 1997. Is this a factual transcription of the events? As my father's son, a professional conjuror, and a man willing to lie to his own parents, I won't swear to it. But it's the version I want to remember.

New Year's Eve 1997

My parents have not been sparkling of late. They laugh less and grouse at each other more. Their view of the world has darkened. This morning my mother made her bed, then opened the blinds and looked out the window onto the wintry Philadelphia street. "People out there are getting conservative," she said. "All the cars are black."

My parents have been artists since the 1930s. They met in art school. And more than sixty years later they still paint. Once a day, for an hour or so, rarely at the same time, Mam and Pad slowly mount the three stories to the art studio. The studio is the joy of their home and painting the one reliable joy in their day. Mam's knees are bad. Sometimes she does the last flight of steps on all fours. She is determination made flesh. Mam works on quiet still lifes in acrylic paint. Pad's eyes are bad, so he does huge wild abstract expressionist paintings in oil. He sees it as a way to turn macular degeneration into a creative tool.

After painting, my parents trudge down from Parnassus to the linoleum-floored kitchen and spend most of their day sitting at the vinyl-cloth-covered table. Mam, tiny, with large, amber-rimmed bifocals, sits elbow on table, forehead resting on hand, staring down. I call it the Posture of Desolation. Pad, his huge bearlike hand rubbing the top of his bald head, squints as he stares at his jumble puzzle in the newspaper with the help of a lighted magnifying glass.

But when I am in town—as I am this New Year's Eve for a weeklong run at the Forrest Theatre—the pace changes. Mam cooks. Nothing stops her. Sure, she finds herself burning broccoli more than in the old days, but she still cooks. Massive meals. Culinary epics. "Cooking. That's what Irene does." Pad sighs. He thinks of the mot juste. "It's her *occupation*."

And truly, the occasional stovetop conflagration aside, Mam is still a great chef. She rarely consults recipes; she just does what she knows makes beautiful food. Around noon she puts a chicken in a small enamel roasting pan, stuffs it with a few cut-up onions and stalks of celery. She plugs up the hole with a wad of stale bread, then shakes bottled seasoning on top. She packs potatoes and peeled carrots on both sides and puts it in the oven at 350 degrees for a couple of hours. When the chicken is on the brink of brown, she turns off the oven and lets it rest for the remainder of the afternoon before reheating and browning it for dinner at 5:00 p.m.

Meanwhile, she sends Pad to the vegetable market for some parsley. She considers parsley essential for the display of the chicken, to contrast with the warm colors of the roast, the potatoes, and the carrots. Mam composes her dinners as she would a still life. Amber acorn squash complements pale-green zucchini. Muted red sweet-and-sour beets pungently balance the dark, bitter turnip greens. I wonder if the instincts that guide artists in color harmony are derived from primeval food-gathering. When Fannie Farmer codified recipes, was it really an advance? Or did she merely introduce paint-by-numbers cooking?

After dinner, I open a package a good friend has sent my parents as a New Year's gift. It contains—among other gifts—three tiaras of red, blue, and magenta feathers with the legend "Happy New Year" in spangles.

When I bring out the tiaras and put mine on, Mam and Pad immediately don theirs. Suddenly, everybody is laughing. We take pictures of one another—and what pictures!

Pad scratching the top of his head like an ape. Mam smiling regally with her lips closed to hide her bad teeth.

Mam, frank as always, looks me in the face and says, "You don't have any idea, do you? Any idea how much you do for us when you're here? I'm not even going to take a nap after dinner," said Mam. "I don't even feel tired . . ."

"Irrational exuberance, that's what it is," Pad remarks.

"Old age," says Mam. "You never know what to expect."

But now it's time for me to go do my show, downtown at the Shubert theater. I've been hoping to lure my parents out of the house to come and see my show later in the run. Whenever I bring this up, Mam starts trembling. She complains that she hasn't been to a proper hairdresser for months, worries about her unpredictable bowels.

I put on my winter coat, and Pad walks me to the door. Pad, who wants to go to the show but won't go if Mam won't, reminds me to pick up the tickets. "I think," he says, "that if we have the tickets in hand, she'll feel like she *has* to go. She won't want to waste them." Ah, waste: secret ally of the progeny of Depression-age parents.

After the show I decline a party invitation and take a cab straight home, with the requested and dreaded tickets in my pocket, the remains of a dressing-room fruit basket in one hand, and a bouquet of a fan's congratulatory white tea roses in the other.

I am surprised to find the vestibule light lit for me, as if I were expected early.

I come in, laden with tickets, basket, and bouquet, and Mam says, "How about that! I just lit the vestibule light and thought I'd stay up for a few extra minutes, and here you are. Oh, look at these things! Pad!"

Pad had been in the living room, napping on the couch. He staggers into the kitchen, foggy. "I'm so weak!" he exclaimed. He rubs his bald head like a surprised Samson. "I've been shorn!"

"You woke up with that joke in your head and that's what dragged you in here, wasn't it?" says Mam.

"No, I thought of it on the way."

Let me tell you, if you want to give your frugal parents gifts, just let them know that somebody gave the gifts to you and they didn't cost a thing. My parents smell and taste everything in the fruit basket without complaining about the price. Mam gushes over the flowers, arranges them in a cut-glass vase her mother bequeathed to her, and does not once reprimand me for overspending.

Then, very tentatively, Mam asks if I'd be willing to have a glass of champagne with them. She knows I will refuse (I'm a teetotaler) and that this little celebratory gesture will have to be omitted. "It's the cheapest stuff," she says, "but, you know, it's supposed to be New Year's."

I think about the probability that this might be our last New Year's Eve as a more-or-less lucid family in the family home, and say, "Okay."

Mam is amazed. For once I'm doing the "right" thing with them on New Year's Eve. With Pad and me spotting her, she wills herself up the step stool to the cupboard above the stove, looking for anything that would pass as a champagne glass. She finds three tallish wineglasses in the back of the cupboard, and I rinse the years of dust off them.

I pop the plastic cork off the bottle of corner-store champagne that has been in the back of their refrigerator for Jesus-knows-how-many years and pour each of us half a glass. We don our feather tiaras and stand in the middle of the kitchen floor, under the fluorescent tube lights, and toast. I say, "Happy New Year." Pad repeats, "Happy New Year." Three months ago I finished building a house in Las Vegas, so Mam's toast celebrates that: "A long and happy life for you in your new home."

Pad drinks. "Phew," he says. "Fizzy vinegar."

"Pfff," I say. It tastes like chilled stomach acid.

Mam makes a lemon-sucking face.

I hand them each a napkin. "Get a load of these," says Pad. "They're the ones you bought at Pathmark. Three-ply. You could take a bath with that."

"You can tell he went through some hard times," Mam observes.

I notice that the New Year's gift package has more stuff in it. There are "Christmas Crackers," those tubes wrapped in paper that set off a cap when you pull a tab in the end and find a present inside. We each take one. Pad gets a tiny plastic top. He tries spinning it with his very big fingers. We laugh. Mam gets a three-quarter-inch-diameter puzzle with two rings to hoop over a peg. The rings were jammed in place. "This is just *junk*," she says, and this is such a mot juste that we all laugh. I get a blue plastic collie the size of a quarter. I say the words "Blue plastic collie," and this strikes Pad as funny, so I keep saying, "Blue plastic collie!"

Upon further examination we find that the crackers also contain slips of paper with jokes in half a dozen languages:

TEACHER: If Shakespeare were alive today,
would he be considered a remarkable man?
PUPIL: Sure, he'd be more than 400 years old.

In what country were you born?
England.
What part?
All of me, silly.

What kind of leather makes the best shoes?
I dunno, but banana peels make the best
slippers.

Well, of course, with a bit of terrible champagne in the blood-
stream, these seem like fine jokes for a party, and we laugh.
Then we discover that what we thought was packing tissue in
the crackers is actually three tissue-paper crowns. So we
drape our feather tiaras with red, yellow, and blue tissue-
paper crowns and take some more photos.

Mam picks up the *TV Guide*. Through her bifocals, she
notices something on the address label. "Pad, just think.
You're going to be getting this guide long after you're dead.
You've paid for it for the next six years."

She hands Pad the remote control to do his job (the remote scares her). Pad turns on the TV. The plump weatherman is predicting a clear day for Philadelphia's traditional
Mummers Parade. Mam points to the weatherman. "I like
him," she says. "He's knowledgeable and amiable. The only
problem is, he takes up too much of the screen."

Pad clicks over to *Dick Clark's New Year's Rockin' Eve*. Dick introduces the Spice Girls. "They're nice," says Pad. "But it's not that hard, what they do. They just wiggle."

Mam replies, "I'd like to see *you* shake your ass like that."

Well, the New Year's countdown happens, and the ball drops and suddenly my father tromps over to my mother, who's seated in the rocking chair, and locks mouths with her with intense determination, ending in a smacking sound.

"There," he says, "that's our annual kiss."

My father comes to me and gives me a hearty handshake.

My mother hobbles over to me with iron determination and kisses me on the head.

Happy New Year from the Teller family kitchen. We of the tissue-paper crowns salute you.

WHEN I READ that entry, I just smile and smile. Remember: When those moments happen, write it all down. It's worth the work, forever.

Five New Year's Eves later I had established myself in a year-round theater run at the Rio All-Suites Hotel in Las Vegas. Once every month, I would shut down my show and fly to Philadelphia for a few days to look in on Mam and Pad. After a year of this, Mam (now ninety-five) and Pad (now ninety) pronounced the monthly trip too much expense and strain on The Kid, and said they'd be willing to move to Las Vegas, to let the family be together for their last years. Still caregiving, but this time by making their caregiver's job less stressful. The guts it took to make this choice still staggers me.

I found and furnished lodgings for Pad and Mam in a homey assisted-living cottage—two bedrooms, two baths, a separate room with north light for an art studio, and twenty-four-hour-a-day help. To shield my parents from the horrors of post-9/11 airport security, I arranged a private jet to transport them. But no fancy plane could conceal the bottom line: My parents were leaving their home.

Mam was wide awake for the last thirty-six hours before their departure. She was determined not to leave anything important behind. She packed boxes with pillows and blankets, stacks of old tax returns, hot pads and toasters. My Jeffersonian "brother," J., stayed at her side. He made sure the essentials were packed and helped the junk get overlooked. Pad slept most of the time, except to wake occasionally and comment, "Throw it all away. Let's get all new stuff out there. That'll be fun."

Finally, the sun rose on the departure day.

Mam, Pad, J., and a cheerful nurse took a van to the plane and boarded. The plane took off. When their own personal flight attendant brought out a beautiful dinner, complete with real French champagne, Mam's anxiety evaporated with the bubbles. When they arrived, Mam and Pad looked ready for a challenge.

Their Vegas lodgings were expensive, but Mam and Pad didn't mind. They were proud that their lifelong frugality had given them the independence to pay their own way, and they insisted on it. Pad calculated that after the sale of their house, they could both have lived to a hundred and never have had to depend on their Kid. Pad consistently evaluated every meal he was served, and complained about the bland artwork in the assisted-living cottage. But that was easy to solve. I offered to hang Mam and Pad's paintings in the halls and dining room, and the other residents were thrilled.

I visited Mam and Pad every afternoon and took art lessons from Pad. "I came out here to die," Pad said between brushstrokes, "but I have four things I want to do first: I want to see the house you built. I want to see your show at the theater they named after you. I want a good seafood dinner. And I want a really tall piece of cake."

Mam visited the art studio often. She sometimes got staff members to pose for pastel portraits. But mostly she made sure Pad was looked after, then enjoyed the sunshine, kept count of the hibiscus flowers on the porch, and gave me grooming advice (almost daily, she suggested I buy a small toupee). Even in her last year, with osteoporosis, ruptured vertebrae, cataracts, arthritis, emphysema, hay fever, bladder problems, and congestive heart failure, she had not lost her ability to wisecrack.

NEW AIDE (UNDERESTIMATING MAM AND POINTING TO ME): "Do you know who that is?"
MAM: "It's the man who meddles in all my affairs."

Nor had Pad lost his edge.

MAM: I'm dying first, like it or lump it.
PAD: Have it your way.

Mam and Pad had a New Year's dinner at my "new" home. I roasted a pork loin by Mam's method (bone in, smothered in onions, cooling-off rest period in the all-day process—the recipe for which is one of the many things I recorded in my book *When I'm Dead All This Will Be Yours*). They saw my show at the Penn & Teller

Theater at the Rio, and gaped at the thirty-foot-high billboard of their Kid's head.

After a year of such gentle adventures, Pad was growing impatient. "I read the obituaries every day, and I'm never there, dammit," he remarked. I knew he couldn't wait too much longer, and I didn't want anything on his list left undone. On his birthday, I made sure he had that really good seafood dinner he had wished for—in a duplex penthouse suite at the Rio with Mam, my friends, and a showgirl in a spangled bikini and feathers. Pad gazed on the showgirl with unabashed joy, and Mam tried on the showgirl's headdress, which was almost as big as she was.

Were my parents fazed by the opulence? Pad sure wasn't. An hour into the party, Pad started yawning, and didn't complain when my crew assisted him up the sweeping staircase to a plush canopy bed for his nap. On his way home afterward, Pad said simply, "That was real good. That was just right."

Mam took it in stride, too. On her birthday, she had her hair done, put on her red outfit and black enamel earrings, and rode regally into a posh Bellagio French restaurant in her wheelchair, with no apparent embarrassment. She chatted with her guests, watched the dancing-fountain show from her dinner table, defiantly downed two glasses of rare port wine, and pronounced her shrimp risotto "delicious!" with the conviction of a lifelong cook.

On my parents' anniversary, I engaged a wonderful close-up magician to entertain them and their friends at the assisted-living cottage, and served a ten-inch-tall chocolate cake. A tall cake. Pad ate his slice with concentration and a hint of relief. He was ready.

So was Mam. I noted this cheerful conversation at her cardiologist's office:

CARDIOLOGIST: "I don't know what's causing your breathlessness, but your heart is actually stronger."

MAM (SMIRKING): "Okay. What can I do to weaken it?"

ALL: (Laugh)

BUT BEFORE DEPARTING there was one final bit of unfinished business. The day the final-notice form for renewing *TV Guide* arrived, I offered to make out a check.

With one voice, my parents told me not to.

But, I said, this would be their last issue.

They told me to throw the form away. They'd outlived the damn subscription. Not an issue would go to waste. Now they could die in peace.

About the Contributors

ALYSIA ABBOTT is a contributing producer on WNYC's *The Leonard Lopate Show*. She previously worked at the New York Public Library and contributed to the anthology *Out of the Ordinary: Essays on Growing Up with Gay, Lesbian, and Transgender Parents*, winner of the 2000 Lamda Literary Award. Her writing has also appeared in *Time Out New York* and Salon.com. She received an MFA in creative nonfiction from New School University and was the winner of its 2003 Chapbook Award. She lives in Brooklyn.

THOMAS BELLER is the author of *The Sleep-Over Artist, Seduction Theory*, and *How to Be a Man: Scenes from a Protracted Boyhood*. A lifelong resident of New York City, he is a cofounder and editor of *Open City* magazine and creator of the website www .mrbellersneighborhood.com.

PETER HO DAVIES, who was born in Britain to Welsh and Chinese parents, is the author of the story collections *The Ugliest House in the World* and *Equal Love*. His work has appeared in *Atlantic Monthly, Harper's, Granta,* and the *Paris Review,* and been selected for *Best American Short Stories* and *Prize Stories: The O. Henry Awards.*

ELIZABETH DEVITA-RAEBURN was fourteen when her older brother, Ted, her only sibling, died of aplastic anemia, a severe immune deficiency disorder. In *The Empty Room: Surviving the Loss of a Brother or Sister at Any Age,* she tells her story and those of some of the seventy-seven bereaved siblings she interviewed. Her articles about science, health, and society have appeared in the *Washington Post, Self, Glamour, Health,* and *Harper's Bazaar.* She holds a master's degree in public health from Columbia University.

LYNN HARRIS is author of the comic novel *Miss Media* and the forthcoming *Death by Chick Lit.* An award-winning journalist, Lynn writes frequently about culture and gender for Salon.com, Nerve .com, *Glamour,* and others. She is a cocreator, with supergenius Christopher Kalb, of the website Breakup Girl (breakupgirl.net) and its television and literary spinoffs. A recovering stand-up co-median, Lynn lives in Brooklyn with her husband.

KATHRYN HARRISON is the author of the novels *Envy, The Seal Wife, The Binding Chair, Poison, Exposure,* and *Thicker Than Water.* She has also written the memoirs *The Kiss* and *The Mother Knot;* a travel memoir, *The Road to Santiago;* a biography, *Saint Thérèse of Lisieux;* and a collection of personal essays, *Seeking*

Rapture. Her writing has appeared in *The New York Times Book Review, The New Yorker, Harper's, Vogue,* and *O* magazine, and on Salon.com. She lives in New York with her husband, the novelist Colin Harrison, and their children.

JOHN HODGMAN is the author of *The Areas of My Expertise.* He lives in New York City, where he curates and hosts "The Little Gray Book Lectures," a monthly colloquium of readings, songs, and dubious scholarship. He is a contributing writer at *The New York Times Magazine* and a frequent voice on public radio's *This American Life,* where he posed this question, among others: "Which superpower would you choose: flight or invisibility?" (The correct answer is invisibility.) Further fiction, nonfiction, and genres in between have appeared in the *Paris Review, McSweeney's, One Story,* and the *Believer.*

MOLLY JONG-FAST is the twenty-seven-year-old author of the novels *Normal Girl* and *Girl (Maladjusted).* She has written for the *New York Times,* the *New York Observer, The Times* of London, *Cosmo, Mademoiselle,* and *Marie Claire.* She holds an MFA from Bennington College, and lives in New York City with her husband, her child, and Pete, the world's fattest cat. Her mother wrote *Fear of Flying,* her grandpa wrote *Spartacus,* and her great-great-grandfather was a herring merchant.

JANICE P. NIMURA's book reviews appear in publications including the *New York Times,* the *Washington Post,* the *Los Angeles Times,* the *Chicago Tribune, Newsday,* and *People.* She lives with her husband and two children in New York City.

Alissa Quart is the author of *Hothouse Kids: The Dilemma of the Gifted Child* and *Branded: The Buying and Selling of Teenagers*. She writes for the *New York Times* and *Film Comment*. She dislikes playing alone.

Sara Reistad-Long is a writer, editor, and reporter based in New York. Her work has appeared in publications such as *Marie Claire, Elle, Glamour, Real Simple, Time Out New York,* and *Lexus*. She is a contributor to *Esquire's Things a Man Should Never Do Past 30*, and has consulted on food-industry trends for Faith Popcorn's Brain Reserve, a national marketing consulting firm.

Amy Richards is currently at work on *Opting In: The Case for Motherhood and Feminism*. She is also the author (with Jennifer Baumgardner) of *Manifesta: Young Women, Feminism, and the Future* and *Grassroots: A Field Guide for Feminist Activism*. In 1992, Amy cofounded the Third Wave Foundation. She is also involved with Planned Parenthood of New York City, the Sadie Nash Leadership Project, and the Lower Eastside Girls Club.

Betty Rollin is the author of *First, You Cry* and *Last Wish*. She is at work on another nonfiction book, which will be published in 2007. She is a contributing correspondent for PBS's *Religion and Ethics Newsweekly* and was formerly a correspondent for NBC News. She lives in New York with her husband, Dr. Harold Edwards, a mathematician.

Ted Rose is a journalist and former television producer whose work has appeared in the *New York Times,* the *Washington Post,* and *Newsweek International,* and aired on National Public Radio's *All Things Considered.* He lives in Boulder, Colorado.

DEBORAH SIEGEL is the author of *Sisterhood, Interrupted.* Her essays and articles on women, sex, contemporary families, and popular culture have appeared in anthologies, academic journals, online, and in magazines such as *Psychology Today* and *The Progressive.* She is a Fellow at the Woodhull Institute for Ethical Leadership and holds a doctorate in English and American literature from the University of Wisconsin–Madison. She lives in New York City.

TELLER is the smaller, quieter half of Penn & Teller. He is the author of *When I'm Dead All This Will Be Yours* and a coauthor, with Penn Jillette, of *Penn & Teller's Cruel Tricks for Dear Friends, Penn & Teller's How to Play with Your Food,* and *Penn & Teller's How to Play in Traffic.* He has written for *The New Yorker, GQ, American Heritage,* the *Atlantic Monthly,* the *New York Times,* and the *Washington Post.* Penn & Teller play nightly in Las Vegas at the Rio All-Suites Hotel.

PETER TERZIAN writes about books for *Newsday* and other publications. He lives in Brooklyn.

JUDITH THURMAN is a staff writer at *The New Yorker* and the author of the prizewinning biography: *Isak Dinesen: The Life of a Storyteller,* which won the National Book Award for nonfiction and was the basis for Sydney Pollack's Oscar-winning film *Out of Africa.*

She is also the author of *Secrets of the Flesh: A Life of Colette*, winner of the Los Angeles Times Book Prize and the Salon Book Award, and a finalist for the Pulitzer Prize. She is completing a volume of her collected essays, *Cleopatra's Nose*. She lives in Manhattan with her son, William.

SARAH TOWERS'S short stories and essays have appeared in *Tin House, Elle, Nerve, The New York Times Book Review, Mirabella, Vogue, Seventeen,* and *BookForum.* She has taught fiction and literature at Boston University and Colgate, and currently teaches creative writing through the Bard Prison Initiative at Eastern State Penitentiary in upstate New York. She is finishing her first collection of stories, titled *On the Universal Tendency Toward Debasement in the Sphere of Love.*

DAPHNE UVILLER is a former editor and a current contributor to *Time Out New York.* Her book reviews, profiles, and articles—on topics ranging from Jewish firefighters to breast reductions—have been published in the *Washington Post,* the *New York Times, Forward, Newsday, Allure,* and *Self,* for which she used to write an ethics column. She lives with her husband and daughter in New York City.

REBECCA WALKER is the author of *Black, White, and Jewish: Autobiography of a Shifting Self* and the editor of *What Makes a Man: 20 Writers Imagine the Future* and *To Be Real: Telling the Truth and Changing the Face of Feminism.* Her work has appeared in *Harper's, Interview, Vibe, Essence, SPIN, Glamour,* and *Buddhadharma,* and on

Salon.com. She is the recipient of the Alex Award from the American Library Association, and fellowships from Yaddo and the MacDowell Colony. She is a cofounder of the Third Wave Foundation, the only national philanthropic organization for women ages fifteen to thirty.

ACKNOWLEDGMENTS

Two only children, both adored daughters. Two writers, both ambitious and prone to obsessive perfectionism. We were two egos waiting to clash. Instead, this book took a friendship and turned it into a beloved sisterhood. We have played beautifully together (if we do say so ourselves), thought as one brain, and triumphed over our childhood aversions to group projects. During the course of creating *Only Child,* we have supported each other through divorce and death, through birth and refinancing. It has been an unmitigated pleasure, from proposal to publication. So first and foremost, we extend heartfelt thanks to each other. Onlies do connect.

Many have buoyed us, and this project, along the way. For sisterly support, writerly company, a keen editorial eye, and for introducing us to each other, our gratitude to Heather Hewett. For encouragement and for space to think, we thank the inspiring women behind the Woodhull Institute for Ethical Leadership, and the Woodhull alumnae community. For keeping us out of the

loony bin and for nurturing our writing and our souls, our gratitude to the ever-wise Robert Berson.

This book was a highly collaborative endeavor. For helping us
in our thoroughly unscientific methods of determining who out
there in the wide world of literature was sibling-free—and still
walking this earth—our gratitude goes to Elizabeth Gilbert, Jay
Jennings, Janice Lee, Rachel Lehman-Haupt, Pamela Paul, Elizabeth Schmidt, Janet Steen, Calvin Trillin, and Helen Whitney. For
early support at the proposal stage, thanks to Debby Carr, Kaja
Perina, and John Burnham Schwartz. For believing in this project
in its nascence, our gratitude to Kim Meisner, and for gracefully
and competently ushering it into adulthood, Julia Pastore and
Kate Kennedy. For his gentle kindness, for always answering our
steady stream of e-mails and phone calls, and for finding us in the
first place, superagent Tracy Brown. Truly, you are a gem among
men. For making this book more poignant and entertaining than
we dared hope it could be, and for making us chortle and weep
along the way, we thank our astoundingly talented contributors.

DEBORAH SIEGEL

Gratitude to my colleagues at the National Council for Research
on Women, whose vision and brilliance sustain me and who gave
me a professional home. Cheers to Rena Uviller and all the Spec-
tors, for a weekend home in Warwick. A belated thank-you to the
late Martha Wood, for imagining the world differently, and to the
late Peggy Lane, who claimed me as Daughter Number Five.
Kudos to my one-of-a-kind book authors' group, for teaching me

the business of writing, with special thanks for solidarity and unparalleled friendship to Katie Orenstein, Annie Murphy Paul, Alissa Quart, and Rebecca Segall—you inspire, and I wouldn't want to be in New York without you. Love and gratitude to distant sisters Rebecca London, who will always tell me what she thinks; Eileen O'Halloran, who helps me listen to what I know; and Busy Zachar, who sent me Troll pajamas. Deep appreciation to Michael Heller, with whom I learned much about how to be two. And to Marco, who reminded me.

   Finally, I thank my extended family: cousins who have moonlighted as sibling stand-ins, especially "big brother" Howard; parental surrogates on the East Coast, Rita and Nick Lenn; my grandmother in Chicago, whose afghans warm my spirit, "mistakes" and all; and my grandparents in Minneapolis, who still share the first article I ever wrote with everyone who stops by. This book is dedicated to my mother, Renée, who was able to both love and let go, and my father, Allen, fellow adventurer in writing and life. "Life is for living." Long may we ski.

DAPHNE UVILLER

This book would not have happened without a veritable army of babysitters. For diaper changes, park visits, and endless games of peekaboo, my thanks to the superb Sara Franklin (can you adopt an eighteen-year-old?), Nan Dale, Ben and Shannon Agin, Ofelia Ariza, Michael Lee, Lucy Schaeffer, and the occasional unwitting staff member at the Center for Biodiversity and Conservation. For being my rock during the most turbulent couple of years I ever could have imagined, my eternal gratitude goes to Paula, Jerome, and Jennie Spector. They create a home and a hearth wherever they go, and though I am generally suspicious of superlatives, they are, hands down, the most generous people I have ever met. I am proud and fortunate to call them my in-laws. I would not be a writer, or an only child, or a writer writing about being an only child, were it not for my mother and father: extraordinary people, extraordinary parents. Mom, from you I learned to brook no artifice and from you I learned empathy. From Daddy, I got the confidence to try my hand at whatever inspired me. He was able to raise a glass of vodka to the sale of this book; arm in arm, Mom, you and I will celebrate, on his behalf, our future accomplishments.

And finally, my boundless appreciation for Sacha Spector: Without you, I would have nothing hanging on my walls, no seasoning in my saucepans, and, of course, no Talia, our grinning, drooling, endless source of fascination and joy. Without your constant, and I mean *daily*, encouragement and cheering, I doubt I would have had the confidence to have kept writing for this long. Without your wisdom, your careful thought, your generosity, and your delicious smile, the world would be a darker place, and I would probably be a consultant, whatever that is.

A NOTE ON THE TYPE

This book was set in Scala, a typeface designed by Martin Majoor in 1991 while working at Utrecht's Vredenburg concert hall in the Netherlands. At the time, there were few fonts available that would print well at small sizes and contained nonlining figures and small capital letters, so he took matters into his own hands and designed his own. Scala is characterized by an even stroke, with letterforms that can claim both French and Dutch ancestry. Majoor added Scala Sans to the family in 1993.